Mathematical Puzzles

And Other Brain Twisters

By Anthony S. Filipiak

BELL PUBLISHING COMPANY • NEW YORK

This edition published by Bell Publishing Company
a division of Crown Publishers, Inc.,
by arrangement with A. S. Barnes and Company, Incorporated
k l m n o p q

Bell 1978 Printing

Library of Congress Cataloging in Publication Data
Filipiak, Anthony S
Mathematical puzzles, and other brain twisters.
First published under title: 100 puzzles, how to
make and how to solve them.
1. Puzzles.   2. Mathematical recreations.   I. Title.
[GV1493.F5 1978]   793.7'3   78-15442
ISBN 0-517-01544-7

This book is dedicated to Master Stephen Edward Filipiak. May he, as he attains to boyhood, youth, and manhood, get as much joy in solving mechanical and manipulative puzzles as he now gets simply from playing with them.

ACKNOWLEDGMENTS

Space does not permit the names of all those who deserve or seek credit for either inventing, creating, or devising the puzzles found in this book. There were times when I was elated over what appeared to be a newly created or devised puzzle, but when paging through one of the many pamphlets, books or periodicals in which appear an occasional puzzle, I would discover that the "new puzzle" had been originated and named by another puzzler. After a few such experiences I came to the conclusion that puzzles are a product of civilization. Nevertheless I wish to acknowledge the help received from the puzzlers of the past, whose puzzle problems are recorded in the annals of antiquity, and from the puzzlers of the present whom I have met, as the saying goes—"Along the highways and byways of America." I wish especially to acknowledge the help received from the following: Mr. Edward Hyde—wire puzzle expert, collector and craftsman of puzzles; Mr. Harold Kittsley —mathematical puzzle enthusiast and collector of mechanical puzzles; Mr. Charles Wedemeyer for his help in compiling and proofreading the manuscript; Mr. John Rashinsky for his assistance in diagramming the puzzles; Mrs. Anthony Filipiak and Master Stephen Filipiak, for the sacrifices they have made in order that a new puzzle be mastered and added to the collection of over a thousand different kinds and types of mechanical and manipulative puzzles.

CONTENTS

PUZZLES

Puzzles are man-created problems that challenge one's ingenuity, initiative, skill, intelligence and patience. Because they are challengers they create a competitive interest whose "pay-off" is not fame and glory but self-satisfaction. Because they are primarily amusements, they teach one to be a good loser. They keep the hands busy and mind active. Puzzles give an outlet to pent up talents and interests which do not have an opportunity to find expression in one's daily vocational pursuits. From a psychological point of view, puzzles are highly educational because they direct one's thinking along logical channels. They neither ask nor demand physical prowess or mental aptitudes, nor are they limited to any age group. The timid and physically handicapped find that puzzles help them to win some degree of recognition and therefore they, in a small measure, help to build confidence.

Puzzles are not seasonal forms of recreation. There is no strenuous physical activity involved. A playing area is not required. The materials for puzzle construction are not expensive, and a craftsman need not be hired to construct the puzzles, for anyone can make them.

The mechanics of puzzles are quickly acquired. Perfection, exactness, and accuracy come with effort expended. The puzzler is not disappointed in the little he gets for the amount of time, effort, and work put forth in finding the solution. Puzzles have a power to create that "pause to refresh" atmosphere because they are enticers to play between work duties.

This book was compiled for those who find enjoyment, entertainment and relief from worry in solving mechanical and manipulative puzzles and for the recreational leader who uses puzzles as a leisure time activity. A few can be purchased—but by including such information the title of the book would be misleading; and furthermore it's more fun to make than buy them.

The puzzles in this book are arranged in units of ten and in order of difficulty so that they may be used as a progressive form or type of entertainment.

Each one of the hundred puzzles has been used on playgrounds, in summer camps, clubs and in other kindred activities throughout the United States. Although they are about a tenth part of the author's collection yet this book presents a recreational product that has been tried and tested by public use.

MATERIALS AND METHODS OF CONSTRUCTION

To make the puzzles in this book one can stock his basement workshop with tools and jigs of every possible description. The best grade of jig saw is a marvelous instrument to use when making the pieces for the burr puzzle; however, a 36-inch band saw does make a nicer job, in that the cut away parts can be removed in one operation. And a sander does make the removal, of that 1/64 part of an inch that causes one of the assembly pieces to bind, an easier job than does a plane or piece of sand paper. And there is nothing like a drill press when making the peg puzzle boards, and a few more of the handicraft tools make puzzle constructing an enjoyable avocation. However, a pocket knife and lumber from a fruit box are all that are necessary. A saw, plane, vise, compass, protractor, square, bevel, drill, file, sand paper, pencil and mitre box do make puzzle construction easier than making them with just a pocket knife but they are not required. They are useful for accuracy and exactness, but many of my most popular puzzles were whittled when time hung heaviest, out of wood that was at the moment available.

The kind of wood used to construct the puzzles herein described is not specific; however, if you want the longest lasting puzzle it is advisable to purchase a good grade of ply wood or one of many hard woods.

A colored puzzle does have more appeal than one without any color, but for practical purposes, stain, shellac or varnish, which, when dried and rubbed with rubbing compound, makes the best decoration. A few of the puzzles demand a color scheme, but don't use paint on any that are of the assembly type.

A puzzle book is usually arranged in the following manner: one half of book is devoted to the puzzle problems, the other half to the answers or solutions. Because I see no benefits in that arrangement and because the title of the book explicitly states—How to Make and How to Solve Them—the solution of the puzzle follows the puzzle problem.

SHIFTING BLOCK PUZZLES

The shifting block puzzle is essentially a muscular puzzle because its solution is dependent upon movement. The solving process is not a very strenuous undertaking but if one uses a finger to move the blocks within the container, to the right, left, up and down, doing this repeatedly, the finger used will develop a muscular strain.

Solutions are furnished for each one of the ten puzzles in this unit but it is advisable for the puzzler to disregard them. The entertaining feature about any puzzle is the competitive spirit that the puzzle creates and the self-satisfaction one receives when the puzzle problem is solved. The shifting block is not a difficult puzzle to understand, its problem and procedure of working is simple, but its solution is quite difficult. However, if one is determined to solve the puzzle a solution will eventually be arrived at. That is the one point in favor of the shifting block puzzle, it may take hours of shifting but eventually a solution will be attained.

MATERIALS AND METHOD OF CONSTRUCTION

The materials used to make this type of puzzle are varied. The container can be made out of apple box-wood or cardboard. Cardboard is satisfactory but experience has proven that a solid object such as wood has more puzzle appeal and more permanency.

Construct the container in the following manner, cut a box wood board according to the size of the base required as indicated on diagram of puzzle. Sand paper both sides of the board. Nail or glue ½ inch strips along the edges of the board. With a lead pencil mark the design of the puzzle and the problem with an arrow pointing toward solution point. When this has been completed, shellac or varnish the container. For ease in shifting blocks, rub the container with rubbing compound.

Construct the shifting blocks either out of apple box-wood or linoleum. Make the blocks according to size of container used. Do not work with fractional parts of an inch. When blocks have been made, sand paper and round-off the corners and edges. When complete apply varnish or shellac.

When puzzle is complete proceed to solve it. It is advisable to use the rubber end of a pencil to shift the blocks around.

Nineteen Block Puzzle

Puzzle: move block #1 to "B" corner or lower right hand corner of container. Blocks must be moved either to right, left, up, or down. Blocks may not be turned around, they must always be moved in a straight line.

Construct the container so that the inside measurements are 3⅛ x 3⅛ inches. The outside measurement is dependent upon the thickness of the outer rim. Glue or nail this outer rim onto the outer edges of the base-board. The additional ⅛ inch is for easier manipulation of the blocks.

Construct the blocks so that 1 block measures 1 inch square, 10 blocks measure 1 inch by ½ inch, 7 blocks measure ½ inch square, 1 block measures ½ inch by 1½ inches. Thickness of blocks is dependent upon the material used.

Cross section view of container.

Solution for the Nineteen Block Puzzle

MOVE BLOCKS NUMBERED (READ DOWN):

4-5 down	9 up & right	10 right	1 down
2 right	1 right	11 up	6 right
3 up	10 right & down	8 right & down	10 up & right
8 up & right	3 down	7 right	7 up
7 right & up	7-8 left	3 up	1 left
6 right	2 left	8 left	6 down
1 down	6 up & left	7 down & left	5 left
3 left	5 up	11 down	4 up
7-8 up	4 right	10 left & down	6 right & down
6 up & right	9 down	6 left	9-6 up
1 right	1 right	1 up	11-13 right
10 up	10 right & up	8-7-11 right	8-12 down
11 left & up	11 right	12 up	2-3 down
12-13 left	3 down	13 left	7-10 left
4-5 down	7-8 down	7-8 left	1 up
6 right	2 left	11 left & down	9-6 left

Solution for the Nineteen Block Puzzle (*continued*)

MOVE BLOCKS NUMBERED (READ DOWN):

11 up	9-10 down	5 down	6-8 down
13 left	7-6 right	17 down	2 right
9-6 right	4 up	1 right	19 up
16 up	5 right	6 right & up	7 up & left
14-15 right	17 up	7 up & right	10 up
12 down	18-19 left	12 right & up	1 left
8 left & down	9-10 down	18 left	6 down
2-3 down	7-6 down	19 up	8 right & down
10 down & left	4 right	10 up & right	10 right
1 left	5 up	9 up	1 up
9 up	7-6 left	4-5 left	6 left
6 left & up	4 down	17 down	8 down & left
11 left	5 right	13-9-10 right	17 up
4-5 down	7-6 up	11 down	4-5 right
9 right	17 right	18-19 left	6 down
6 up & right	8 right & down	1 down	8 left & down
1 right	1 down	8-6 right	1 down
10 right & up	7 left	7-12 up	7 right
2-3 up	6 up & left	19 up	19 down
8 up & right	17 up	18 right	2 left
12 up	8 right & up	11 up	10 up & left
16 down	17-18 up	13 left	17 up
11 left & down	9 left	18 left	5 up
1 down	10 down & left	9 left & up	4 right
7-10 right	4 down	10 left	8 right & down
2-3 up	5 down	1 down	1 down
8-12 up	17 right	19 right	7 down & left
11-13 left	8 up	7-12 down	10 down
4-5 down	1 right	2 right	17 left
6-9 down	7 down	3 up	5 up
7-10 right	6 left & down	11 up	4 up
1 up	8 left	18 left	8 right & up
12-8 right	1 up	12 down	6 right
11 up	18 up	11 right	1 down
13 right	19 up	12-9 left	10 down & left
12-8 left	10 up & left	11-7 down	4 left
4-5 left	4 left	19 left	8-6 up
			1 right

Solved in 213 moves

Nine Block Puzzle

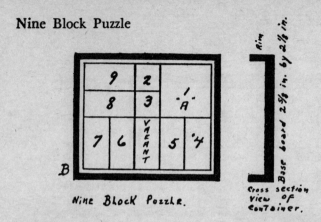

Nine Block Puzzle.

Cross section view of Container.

Puzzle: move block "A" to "B" corner. Blocks must be moved in a straight line.

Construct the container so that its inside measurements are $2\frac{5}{8}$ inches by $2\frac{1}{8}$ inch.

Construct the blocks so that 1 block measures 1 inch square, 2 blocks measure $\frac{1}{2}$ inch square, 6 blocks measure $\frac{1}{2}$ inch by 1 inch.

Solution for the Nine Block Puzzle

MOVE BLOCKS NUMBERED (READ DOWN):

2 & 3 down	6 & 7	2 under 3	1
1	2 above 3	8 & 9	3 & 2
4	6	6	4 & 5
5	7	7	9
2 right	2 & 3	1	8
1	6	5	1
9	7	4	3 above 2
8	3 right of 2	2 & 3	7
6 & 7	9	3 left of 2	6
2 & 3	8	4	1
1	3 & 2	5	
9	9	9	
8	8	8	

Solved in 59 moves

Five Block Puzzle

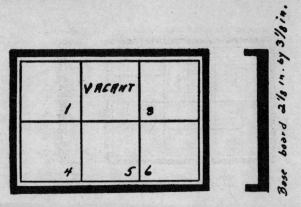

Base board 2⅛ in. by 3⅛ in.

Puzzle: by moving blocks, reverse the #3 and the #6 blocks. That is, move #3 block to #6 corner and #6 block to #3 corner.

Construct the container so that its inside measurements are 2⅛ inches by 3⅛ inches. The additional ⅛ inch for easier manipulation of the blocks.

Construct the blocks so that they measure 1 inch square. Five blocks are used. To make this puzzle more interesting paint #3 green and #6 red. Then the problem can be stated as follows:—Reverse the colored blocks. If you follow the number scheme, paint or carve the numbers 1-2-3-4-5-6 on base of container. If you follow the color scheme paint the 5 and 6 squares, red and green respectively.

Solution for the Five Block Puzzle

MOVE BLOCKS NUMBERED:

3-6-5-3-1-4-3-5   6-1-5-3-4-5-1-6-3

Solved in 17 moves ·

Eleven Block Puzzle

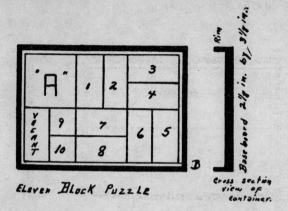

ELEVEN BLOCK PUZZLE

Cross section view of container.

Puzzle: move block "A" to "B" corner. Blocks must always be moved in a straight line.

Construct container so that its inside measurements are 2⅛ inches by 3⅛ inches.

Construct the eleven blocks so that 1 block measures 1 inch square, 2 blocks measure ½ inch square, 8 blocks measure 1 inch by ½ inch.

Solution for the Eleven Block Puzzle

MOVE BLOCKS NUMBERED (READ DOWN):

9 left and down	4	6	4	1	6
7	5	9 over 10	10	7	5
8	6	6	9	8	7
10	10	5	3	A	8
9	9	9	4	9	A
7	1	10	10	10	2
8	2	6	9	1	1
1	3	5	3	2	10
2	4	10 left of 9	4	3	9
3	5	3	2	4	2

Solution for the Eleven Block Puzzle (*continued*)

MOVE BLOCKS NUMBERED (READ DOWN):

1	7	5	A	9	9 left of 10
9 right of 10	5	6	4	A	A
4	6	9	3	4	4
3	9	10	2	3	3
9	10	A	1	2	5
10	4	8	8	1	6
4	3	7	7	8	9
3	A	5	6	7	10
A	8	6	5	6	A
8	7	10 under 9	10	5	

Solved in 119 moves

Bull's-Eye Puzzle—11 blocks

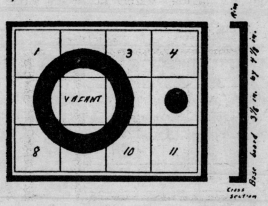

Cross Section

Puzzle: move block with "Bull's-Eye" into center of the target.

Construct the container so that its inside measurements are 3⅛ inches by 4⅛ inches.

Construct the eleven blocks so that each one measures 1 inch square. Paint the circle on the 8 blocks as shown, and paint a round spot on one of the blocks. It is also advisable to paint a "Bull's-Eye" on base of container.

Solution for the "Bull's Eye" Puzzle

MOVE BLOCKS NUMBERED (READ DOWN):

6 left	6 left	2 & 1 right	9 & 7 left
10 up	8 & 5 up	8 & 6 down	11 up
8 & 9 right	1 right	5 left	6 & 1 right
1 & 5 down	6 & 2 down	10 & 2 up	9 down
2 left	8 left	6 right	7 left
6 & 8 up	5 up	5 & 8 down	6 up
5 right	10 left	10 left	1 left
2 & 1 down	9 up	2 up	

Solved in 43 moves

George Washington's Career Puzzle—15 pieces

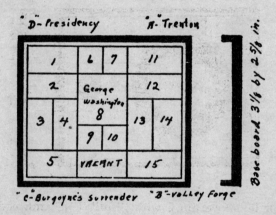

Puzzle: retrace Washington's career by moving large block to the following corners or points in his career:

A—Trenton
B—Valley Forge
C—Burgoyne's Surrender
D—Presidency.

Construct the container so that its inside measurements are 3⅛ inches by 2⅝ inches. The outside measurement is dependent upon the size of the rim used. The additional ⅛ inch is for easier manipulation of the blocks.

Construct blocks so that: 1 block measures 1 inch square, 10 blocks measure 1 inch by ½ inch, 4 blocks measure ½ inch square.

Thickness of blocks is dependent upon material used. Paint the points of Washington's career on base of box.

Solution for the George Washington's Career Puzzle
(15 pieces)

MOVE BLOCKS NUMBERED (READ DOWN):

15 left	11-12 left	8 up	13-14 up
13-14 down	6 left & down	13-14 up	11-5 up
11-12 down	7 left	9-10 right	9-10 left
6-7 right	8 down	5 down	8 down
8 up	1 right	6 down & left	11 right
12 left	2 up	13-14 left	6-7 right
11 down	7 up & left	10 up	15 up
6 down & right	6 up	9 right & up	5 left
8 right	10-11 right	5-11 right	7-9 down
1-2 right	10 right & up	12-15 down	15 right
3 up	5 up	7 left	5 up
4 left	15 left	6 up & left	12 up
9 left & up	11-12 down	13-14 left	9-10 left
10 left	9-10 right	10 left & down	6-7 down
12 down	5-15 up	8 down	15 down
11 left	12 left	1 right	5 right
6 down & left	11 down	2 up	12 up
7 down	9-10 down	13-14 up	9-10 up
8 right	5 right	11 up	6-7 left
1-2 right	15-12 up	5 left	15 down
3 right	11 left	8-9-10 down	5 down
4 up	9-10-5-7-6-2 down	1 down	2 right
9-10 left	1 left	2 right	9 up & left

Solution for the George Washington's Career Puzzle
(15 pieces) *(cont'd)*

3 down	10 up & right	5-15 right	6 left
4 right	13 up	7 down	2-12-15-5 down
9-10-7 up	14 left	9 left & down	1-11 right
6 left & up	8 left	5-15 left	3-4 up
3-4 down	6 down	9 down	7 up & right
9 right	7 right & down	3-4 down	9 up
10-6-7 up	9 right	1-11 left	8 left
3 left	10 down & right	2-12 up	6-10 left
4 down	13 right	6-10 up	13 down
6 right & up	14 up	8 right	14 right
12 left	8 left	5-15 right	7 right & up
13-14 down	10 down	7-9 down	4 right
9-10 right	9 left & down	3-4 down	8 up
6-7 up	2-12 down	1 down	6 left
1-2-3-4 up	11 right	11 left	10 down & left
15 left	13-14 up	13-14 up	13 left
5 down	12 left	5-15 up	14 down
13-14 down	12 right	7-9 right	9 right
1 left	13-14 down	3-4 down	7 up
2 down	11 left	15 left	13-14 up
6-7-9-10 right	2-12 up	5 up	5 left
12 up	7 up & right	7 up & left	15 down
1 left	9 up	8 left	11-2-12 down
2 left	8 right	1 down	1 right
9-10 down	14 down	10 right & down	7-9-13-14 up
6-7 right	13 left	5-15 right	5 up
2 right	7 left & up	3-4 up	15 left
1 up	6 left	7 left	1-11-2-12 down
3-4 up	2-12 down	9 down & left	7-9 right
15 up	11 right	8 left	13-14 up
5 left	7 left & up	10 left & down	5-15 up
13-14 down	9 up	5 down	6-10 right
11 left	13 right	15 right	8 down
6-7-9-10 down	7 down	13-14 down	5 left
12 right	9 left & down	11 right	15 up
2-11 up	1 right	1 up	6-10 up
9-10 left	3-4 up	3-4 up	12 left
6-7-12 down	7 left	7 up & left	11-2 down
2 right	9 down & left	8 left	15 right
11 up	14 up	10 left & up	11 left

Solution for the George Washington's Career Puzzle
(15 pieces) *(cont'd)*

1-15 down	14 up	6 left	9 down
6 down & right	13 right	9 up & left	3-14 left
13-14 right	7 up	13 left	13 up
6 up	3-4 left	14 down	4 right
10 left & up	6 down	3 right	6-7 right
5 right	10 left & down	7 up	7 down
3-4 down	6 right	6-14 up	6 right
6 left	10 down	8 up	11 left
10 up & left	3 left	11 left	7 down & right
13-14 left	7 left & down	13-14 down	6 down
6 left & up	4 up	3-4 down	14 down
1 up	6 right	10-9 right	3 right
5 right	5 down	6-7 up	7 right & up
13-14 down	4 left	11 up	8 up
6-10 left	13 down	3-14 up	11 up
1-5-2-15 up	14 right	4-13 up	6-7 left
12 right	4 right	11 right	4-14 down
11 down	3 right	8 down	7-10 right
13-14 down	10 up	6-9 down	8 up
7 down & left	7 left & up	6 left	

Solved in 465 moves

Ten Block Puzzle

Puzzle: move block "A" to "B" corner, and block "B" to "A" corner. A simpler direction would be: reverse blocks "A" and "B." Blocks must be moved in a straight line.

Construct the container so that its inside measurements are 2⅛ inches by 2⅝ inches. The additional ⅛ inch is for easier manipulation of the blocks.

Construct the blocks so that 2 blocks measure 1 inch square, 2 blocks measure 1 inch by ½ inch, 6 blocks measure ½ inch square.

Color block "A" red. Color block "B" blue. Paint "A" corner of container red and "B" corner of container blue, then directions for working puzzle would be, reverse the colors.

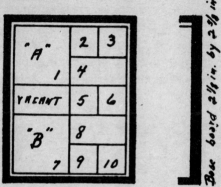

Solution for the Ten Block Puzzle

MOVE BLOCKS NUMBERED (READ DOWN):

5 & 6 left	8 up	9 left & down	3 right & up
2 down & right	9 up & right	1 down	7 up
1 right	7 right	5 down & right	10 up & right
5 up	2 down	4 & 8 right	1 left
6 left & up	3 left & down	2 up	6 down
4 left	8 left	3 left & up	5 right & down
2 down & left	1 down	7 up	4 & 8 down
3 down	5 & 6 right	9 & 10 left	2 & 3 right
1 right	4 & 8 up	1 down	7 up
6 right & up	3 up & right	5 down & left	10 up & right
4 up	2 up	6 down	9 up
2 & 3 left	7 left	4 & 8 right	1 left

Solved in 55 moves

Fifteen Block Puzzle or 1-2-3 Puzzle

Puzzle: move block "L1" to "L3" corner, and block "L3" to "L1" corner. Blocks must be moved in a straight line.

Construct the container so that its inside measurement is 3⅛ square inches. The additional ⅛ inch is for easier manipulation of the blocks.

Construct the blocks so that 3 blocks measure 1 inch square, 2 blocks measure ½ inch square, 10 blocks measure ½ inch by 1 inch.

The blocks need not be numbered, colored blocks are very practical; however, if you color them, paint the container areas with their respective colors.

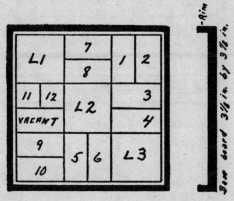

Solution for the 1—2—3 Puzzle

MOVE BLOCKS NUMBERED (READ DOWN):

11-12 down	10 left	3-4 down	4 left
7-8 left	L 1 down	5-6 down	3 up
6 left	11 down & left	7 right	11-12 right
5 up	3-4 left	8 up	4 down
L 1 right	1 up	L 2 up	3 left
11 right & up	2 right	9-10 up	11 up & right
L 2 up	L 1 right	11-12 left	6 down
9 left	11-12 down	3-4 down	5 left
10 down	3-4 left	5-6 down	11-12 up
L 1 down	1 left	7 down	6 right
11-12 right	2 up	8 right	5 down
L 2 up	L 1 right	L 2 up	12 left & up
9 up	12 right & down	9-10 up	10 right

Solution for the 1—2—3 Puzzle (*continued*)

9 down	9-10 left	11-12 up	1-2 down
L 2 down	1 left	9 right	3-4 down
8 left	2 down	10 right	12 down & right
7 up	7-8 right	L 1, L 2 down	L 3 right
11-12 up	L 2 right	7 down	5 up
10 up	12 right & up	8 left	6 left
9 right	L 3 up	3-4 up	3-4 left
L 2 down	9 left	5-6 up	11-12 down
8 down	10 down	11-12 left	L 3 right
7 left	L 2 down	9 up	5 right
11 up & left	12 up & left	10 right	6 up
L 3 left	L 2 left	11 down & right	3-4 left
2 up	6 up	6 down	11 left & down
1 right	5 right	5 left	3 right
9-10 right	9-10 right	11-12 up	4 up
11-12 down	11-12 down	6 right	11-12 left
L 3 left	L 2 left	5 down	3 down
2 left	6 left	11-12 left	4 right
1 up	5 up	L 3 left	12 above 11
9-10 right	9-10 right	2 down	5 down
11 right & down	12 right & down	1 right	6 right
L 3 down	9 left	3-4 right	11-12 up
7 right	10 up	11-12 up	5 left
8 up	11-12 right	L 3 left	6 down
L 2 up	9 down	2 left	12 right & down
11-12 right	10 left	1 down	8 right
L 3 down	5-6 down	3-4 right	7 up
7 down	3 left	11 right & up	11-12 left
8 right	4 up	L 3 up	8 down
L 2 up	L 3 up	5-6 up	7 right
12 up & left	11-12 right	10 left	12 up & left
L 3 left	9 right	9 down	7-8 left
9-10 left	10 down	1-2 down	6 up
1 down	L 1, L 2 down	3-4 down	5 right
2 right	7 left	11-12 right	L 1 right
7-8 right	8 up	L 3 up	11-12 right
L 2 right	3 up	5-6 up	L 3 up
11-12 up	4 left	10 up	9 up
L 3 left	L 3 up	9 left	10 left
			L 2 down

Solved in 262 moves

Rectangle Puzzle

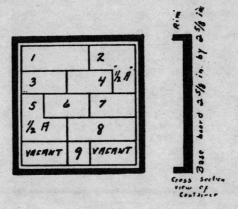

Puzzle: move blocks so as to bring the two ½A's to-gether to make a rectangle in the upper right hand corner of container. Blocks must always be moved in a straight line.

Construct the container so that its inside measurement is 2⅝ inches by 2⅝ inches. The additional ⅛ inch is for easier manipulation of the blocks. Thickness of blocks is dependent upon material used.

Construct blocks so that: 2 blocks measure 1½ inches by ½ inch, 4 blocks measure 1 inch by ½ inch, 1 block measures ½ inch square, 2 blocks measure 1 inch square, with ½ inch square removed from one of the corners.

Solution for the Rectangle Puzzle

MOVE BLOCKS NUMBERED (READ DOWN):

9 left	join 2 & 5 to	9 right
8 down	make rectangle	7 down
7 down	9 down	9 down
6 right	4 left	6 left & **down**
5 right	2 up	4 left
9 left & up	5 right join 2	8 up
8 left	4 right	2 up
7 down	6 right	5 right
6 down	9 up	9 right & down
4 down	8 up	7 up
2 down	7 left	9 left
1 right	5 down	5 left & up
3 up	2 down	7 down & right
9 up	4 right	4 down to bottom
5 left	6 up	3 down to bottom
4 left & up	5 left	1 left
6 left up & left	2 down	8 left
2 down	8 right	2 up to top
4 right	7 down	5 right & up

Solved in 56 moves

Twenty-Seven Block Puzzle

Puzzle: By moving the twenty seven blocks rearrange them into an alphabetical order. Move blocks in a straight line. This puzzle is similar to the "Famous 15" shifting block puzzle.

Construct the container so that its inside measurements are $3\frac{1}{8}$ inches by $2\frac{5}{8}$ inches. The additional $\frac{1}{8}$ inch is for easier manipulation of the blocks. Thickness of blocks is dependent upon the material used.

Construct the blocks so that: 26 blocks measure $\frac{1}{2}$ inch square, 1 block measures $\frac{1}{2}$ inch by $1\frac{1}{2}$ inches.

If you are not desirous of making the blocks for this puzzle, you may purchase a set of anagram blocks from any 5 and 10¢ store, or from stores which handle play equipment.

When constructing puzzle, mark base of container as per diagram; one need not arrange them as shown on diagram but this arrangement has been most satisfactory. Another puzzle would be to reverse the alphabetical order and then by moving blocks arrange them into an alphabetical sequence.

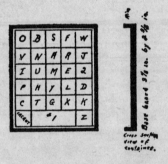

Solution for the Alphabet Puzzle

MOVE BLOCK LETTERED:

#1-X-G-Y-L-D-K-G-Y-T-C-P
H-C-T-L-D-K-2-E-M-D-C-U
N-A-D-C-K-M-R-J-E-R-J-F
W-E-R-J-F-W-S-B-A-O-A-B
D-C-F-W-S-D-C-F-W-J-R-S
J-R-2-G-G-Z-X-Y-M-G-2-S
J-R-G-M-L-T-U-K-W-N-V-F
R-G-N-R-G-N-R-V-I-H-K-W
V-I-H-O-F-G-N-R-I-H-O-F
G-N-H-O-N-H-R-I-O-R-H-G
F-K-P-U-W-V-M-L-T-W-V-M
R-N-M-R-L-2-S-W-V-M-L-T
W-V-M-R-N-M-R-L-2-S-Z-T
Y-#1-U-P-2-R-S-Z-T-Y-W-V
P-2-R-S-Z-T-Y-W-V-Z-S-R
2-P-Z-V-W-Y-T-S-R-2-P-U
#1-X-Y-T-S-R-2-P-U-Z-V-W
X-#1-Z-U-P-2-R-S-T-Y

Solved in 214 moves

STRAIGHT LINE PEG PUZZLES

The straight line peg puzzles are similar to the circle peg puzzles, but in respect to the men who have in the course of civilization made this contribution to man's leisure moments, it is advisable to keep the puzzles as they were originally devised, and created.

The line puzzles can be worked without any special equipment. All one needs to do is to draw on paper two parallel lines, one inch apart, subdividing the lined area into as many one inch squares as puzzle demands and then using buttons, stones or other objects for markers and proceed to solve the puzzle. But because this haphazard method of play is not very satisfactory, it is advisable to make the puzzles out of one inch wide box wood strips. Into these strips drill as many ¼ inch holes as is required for the puzzle. Sandpaper the wood strips, then apply shellac or varnish. While varnish on wood strips is drying make as many ¼ inch wood pegs as are required for the puzzle.

If you make the puzzle out of wood, you will find that it will be used more often than one drawn on paper. However, don't be discouraged by my insistence that puzzles be made of wood. Play them any way you see fit. Puzzles will give you loads of fun and enjoyment, no matter how you construct and play them.

Eight Peg Puzzle

Materials and method of constructing the Eight Peg Puzzle:

Use a wood strip 1 inch by 9 inches. With a compass mark off nine points. At the points marked drill nine ¼ inch holes. Make eight pegs ¼ inch by 1 inch. Paint four any color desired; varnish or stain the remaining four. Place the four colored pegs in the four right holes, and the stained four pegs into the four holes on the left side.

Puzzle: By moving reverse the colors of the pegs. Move by either jumping to the next hole or jumping over one peg. Backward moves are not permitted.

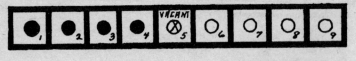

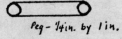

Peg – ¼in. by 1 in.

Solution for the Eight Peg Puzzle

Move left.	Jump right.	Jump left.	Move left.
Jump right.	Jump right.	Jump left.	Jump left.
Move right.	Jump right.	Move right.	Jump left.
Jump left.	Move right.	Jump right.	Move right.
Jump left.	Jump left.	Jump right.	Jump right.
Move left.	Jump left.	Jump right.	Move right.

Solved in 24 moves

Three Colored Pegs Puzzle

Materials and method of constructing the "Three Colored Pegs Puzzle":

Use a 1 inch thick strip of wood, 1 inch wide by 3 inches long. With a ruler or compass mark three points equidistant from each other. At these points drill three ¼ inch holes. Make 3 pegs ¼ inch by 1 inch in length. A strip of wood 3 inches long by 1 inch square is best for this puzzle because with a thick block of wood the colored pegs are not as confusing as they are with a thin piece of wood. Color the pegs so that one half of peg is black, the other half red. Then place two pegs into the outer holes so that the red ends are out of the board; place the third peg into center hole so that the black end is protruding.

Puzzle: In three moves and only three moves—moving two pegs at a time—have either all the red or black ends protruding. Only one color must be above surface of the block.

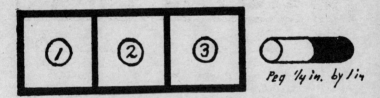

Peg ¼ in. by 1 in.

Solution for the Three Colored Pegs Puzzle

Move and turn over peg 2 and 3,
Move and turn over peg 1 and 3,
Move and turn over peg 2 and 3.

Six Colored Pegs Puzzle

Materials and method of constructing the Six Peg Puzzle:

Use a piece of wood 1 inch wide by 7 inches long. With a compass or ruler mark off seven points equidistant from each other. Make six pegs ¼ inch by 1 inch. Color three with any desired color; stain the other three. Arrange pegs as per diagram.

Puzzle: By moving one peg at a time, reverse pegs and position of empty hole from left to right side. Jump over one or two, but no more than two pegs. Moves may be either to right or left.

Solution for the Six Colored Pegs Puzzle

MOVE PEG NUMBER (READ DOWN):

4 to 1	2 to 1	6 to 3	1 to 4
5 to 4	5 to 2	7 to 6	3 to 1
3 to 5	3 to 5	4 to 7	6 to 3
6 to 3			7 to 6

Solved in 14 moves

Eight Colored Pegs Puzzle

Materials and method of constructing the Eight Colored Pegs Puzzle:

Use a wood strip 1 inch wide by 10 inches long. With a compass or ruler mark off ten points equidistant from each other. Drill ten ¼ inch holes at the points marked. Make eight round pegs ¼ inch by 1 inch. Color four any desired color; stain the other four pegs. Place pegs on board as per diagram.

Puzzle: In four moves, moving two pegs at one time, have pegs alternate in color. That is, one colored, the other stained, and so on. ·

O₁ O₂ O₃ O₄ ●₅ ●₆ ●₇ ●₈ VACANT⊗₉ VACANT⊗₁₀

Peg ¼ in. by 1 inch.

Solution for the Eight Colored Pegs Puzzle

2 and 3 to holes 9 and 10
5 and 6 to holes 2 and 3
8 and 9 to holes 5 and 6
1 and 2 to holes 8 and 9.

Sixteen Ring Puzzle

Materials for Sixteen Ring Puzzle:
One piece of wood 1 inch wide by 16 inches long;
Sixteen ½ inch washers or celluloid rings; however, one inch washers are easier to handle. The celluloid rings can be purchased in any 5 & 10¢ store.
Sixteen 1 inch wire brads or finishing nails.
To construct puzzle: On the wood strip mark off distances with a compass or ruler 1 inch apart. At points marked, place a nail into the wood strip. On each nail place a washer or ring.
Puzzle: By passing a washer over four washers, arrange the sixteen washers into four piles. Do not count the nails; count only the washers.

Ring
Nail or
Wire Brad
Nail

Solution for the Sixteen Ring Puzzle

MOVE RING NUMBERED (READ DOWN):

7 to peg 2	10 to peg 15	14 to peg 16	3 to peg 1
8 to peg 7	6 to peg 10	13 to peg 14	4 to peg 3
9 to peg 8	5 to peg 6	12 to peg 13	11 to peg 4

Solved in 12 moves

Six Colored Pegs Line Puzzle

Materials and method of constructing the six colored pegs puzzle:

Use a ½ inch board four inches wide by six inches long. Mark off points as per diagram. At points marked, drill ¼ inch holes. After sanding the board, connect these holes with heavy pencil lines as per diagram. Color three of the holes either with pencil marks or with paint. To make the pencilled lines permanent, shellac or varnish the board. Make six wood pegs ¼ inch in diameter by 1 inch long. Color three of the pegs and stain the other three. Place the three colored pegs into three of the colored holes and the stained pegs into the three holes on the opposite end of the board.

Puzzle: By moving the pegs, one at a time along any one line toward another hole, reverse the position of the pegs. No jumps are permitted. Fewest number of moves determine the solution of the puzzle. Most puzzles of this type are solvable, but it is the fewest possible moves that make it difficult. However, don't allow this objective to be a hindrance. Practise will make perfection; and don't try to remember the moves on your first attempt.

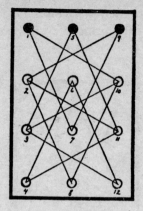

Solution for the Six Colored Pegs Line Puzzle

MOVE PEG NUMBER (READ DOWN):

4 to 6	6 to 12	7 to 9	9 to 2
9 to 2	2 to 11	12 to 3	3 to 5
3 to 10	10 to 1	11 to 4	12 to 3
4 to 6	6 to 12	5 to 11	11 to 4
7 to 9	8 to 10	10 to 1	1 to 7
1 to 7			2 to 8

Solved in 22 moves

Twelve Colored Pegs Line Puzzle

Use the same board as was made for the six colored pegs line puzzle.

Make pegs as per diagram. This type of peg is used so that the letter of the alphabet can be more readily and easily drawn on the head of the peg. However, you need not draw the letters on the head of the peg; you can glue them on as easily. Color six of these pegs any color desired and stain the other six pegs. Place the pegs on the board as per diagram.

Puzzle: By exchanging a colored peg for a stained peg arrange the pegs from left to right into an alphabetical sequence.

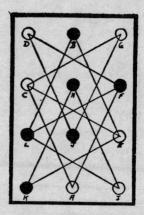

Solution for the Twelve Colored Pegs Line Puzzle

EXCHANGE THE PEGS IN THE FOLLOWING MANNER (READ DOWN):

H for K	I for L	G for J	D for K
H for E	I for F	J for A	E for F
H for C	I for D	F for K	E for D
H for A	K for L	L for E	E for B
			B for K

Solved in 17 moves

E Peg Puzzle

Materials required and method of constructing the E peg puzzle.

Use a ½ inch board four inches wide by five inches long. On this board draw a letter "E." Divide the body and arms into equal parts as per diagram. In the center of these twelve squares drill ¼ inch holes as per diagram. Color the top arm of the letter "E" red, the bottom arm green. Leave center squares uncolored. Make eight pegs ¼ inch in diameter by 1 inch in length. Color four of the pegs red and four green. Set up puzzle as shown on diagram.

Puzzle: By moving pegs into open holes reverse the colored pegs so that the red pegs be on the green arm and the green pegs be on the red arm.

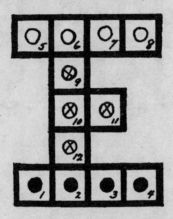

Solution for the E Peg Puzzle

MOVE NUMBERED PEGS INTO NUMBERED HOLES, AS FOLLOWS (READ DOWN):

(1)	(2)	(3)	(4)
6 to 11	4 to 5	1 to 11	3 to 11
2 to 6	7 to 10	2 to 2	6 to 1
1 to 9	8 to 9	7 to 12	2 to 2
3 to 12	4 to 8	1 to 5	5 to 12
4 to 1	8 to 7	7 to 11	3 to 7
3 to 12	7 to 5	2 to 6	5 to 11
6 to 2	8 to 11	6 to 9	2 to 6
4 to 11	5 to 7	3 to 12	6 to 9
1 to 1	2 to 6	8 to 4	5 to 1
2 to 2	1 to 9	3 to 1	6 to 2
5 to 12	8 to 1	7 to 3	

Solved in 43 moves

Thirteen Peg Puzzle

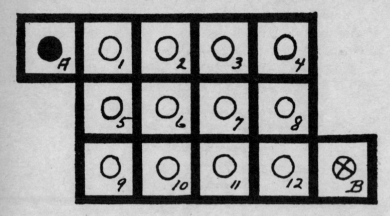

Materials and method of constructing the thirteen peg puzzle:

Use a board six inches long by three inches wide. Divide this board into fourteen squares as per diagram. In the center of these fourteen squares drill ¼ inch holes. Make thirteen pegs ¼ inch in diameter by 1 inch long. Stain one of the pegs. Set up puzzle as shown on diagram.

Puzzle: Remove the uncolored pegs by jumping over one peg and removing peg jumped over, leaving the stained peg on the board in the same position as placed before proceeding to solve the puzzle.

Solution for the Thirteen Peg Puzzle

MOVE PEG NUMBERED (READ DOWN):

11 to B remove 12	4 to 12 remove 8	2 to 1 remove 12
9 to 11 " 10	A to 4 " 1 & 3	10 to 5 ." 4 & 11
2 to 10 " 6	12 to 3 " 7	4 to A " 3 & 1

Sixteen Peg Puzzle

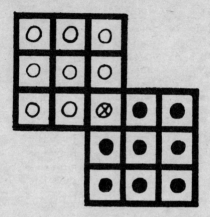

Materials and method of constructing sixteen peg puzzle:

Use a board five inches wide by five inches long. Draw a diagram on it as per design. In the center of these seventeen squares drill ¼ inch holes. Make sixteen pegs ¼ inch in diameter by 1 inch long. Color eight pegs red, and eight black. For a more effective puzzle color one half of board red, the other half black. When board and pegs are dry arrange the pegs on board as per puzzle diagram.

Puzzle: By moving pegs either vertically or horizontally (diagonal moves not permitted) reverse the colors of the pegs. That is, move red pegs to black side of puzzle, and black pegs to red side of puzzle board. Move pegs either one space, into an empty hole or over one peg, but no more than one space or over more than one peg.

Solution for the Sixteen Peg Puzzle

MOVE PEGS (READ DOWN):

Move right	Move right	Move down	Jump down
Jump left	Jump left	Jump down	Jump right
Move left	Move down	Jump right	Jump right
Jump right	Jump right	Move up	Move left
Move up	Move up	Jump down	Jump left
Jump down	Jump down	Jump left	Move right
Move down	Move right	Jump up	Jump up
Jump up	Move up	Move right	Move down
Jump right	Jump down	Jump left	Jump down
Move left	Move left	Jump up	Move up
Jump left	Jump up	Move right	
Move up	Jump up	Jump left	

Solved in 46 moves

CIRCLE PEG PUZZLES

The circle peg puzzle is similar to the straight line peg puzzle except that its problem is somewhat different and it has more puzzle appeal. If this were a textbook on the psychology of puzzles or on methods of teaching that branch of low organized games concerned with quiet games, puzzles, stunts, and tricks, I would elucidate on puzzles as a form of entertainment and its psychology. But due to this being a book of puzzles I merely state that even though there is similarity in playing peg puzzles, yet each type has its place and therefore the most appeal when used in the traditional manner. As for instance the 13 peg circle puzzle or 10 peg circle puzzle will not take as a straight line puzzle because it is customary and traditional to play "count out" in a circle formation. Other reasons could be enumerated but this book is supposed to be concerned primarily with the making and solving of puzzles, therefore;

When making this type of puzzle use a ¾ inch board; the sides of an apple box are very excellent material. Cut it to size and sandpaper both sides so that the puzzle can be placed anywhere without marring fine surfaces.

After the board is sanded use a compass to draw a circle and a protractor to divide the circle into equal parts. If a compass or protractor is not available use a plate, cup, saucer or other round object to make the circle, and in place of the protractor make a circle on a sheet of paper, subdivide it into four parts, then eight, next sixteen and you will have a fairly accurate protractor. Of course you will have to do a little calculating to get your points accurately placed but remember that a puzzle need not be perfectly accurate to have puzzle appeal. After you have your points marked off, drill holes at points. Size of hole dependent upon size of wood pegs used. For ordinary puzzle play, match sticks serve a good purpose. However, if you are a recreational worker and plan to use the board in connection with your work then it is advisable that pegs be at least $\frac{1}{4}$ inch in diameter.

When puzzling don't endeavor to encourage a person to puzzle. Rather give the participant an opportunity to play because he wishes to do so; this can be done by challenging a person to do a certain puzzle in a certain way.

Ten Colored Pegs Circle Puzzle

Materials and methods of constructing the ten peg puzzle:

Use a four inch square board. On it draw a three inch circle. Subdivide the circle into ten equal parts. At points marked off, drill ten $\frac{1}{4}$ inch holes. Make ten $\frac{1}{4}$ inch by 1 inch pegs. Color five of the pegs; the other five can be left in their natural state. Set up puzzle as per diagram.

Puzzle: What numbers when used as in playing the game of "Count and Take Out" will eliminate all of the colored pegs, and what number will eliminate all of the uncolored pegs? As for instance, if you decide to use the number 14, start counting at peg number 1 and

you'll eliminate peg number 4. Then start counting at
the next peg, in this case number 5 and number 14
will fall on number 9. Continue doing this until all of
the colored pegs are removed. The pegs removed are
not counted. If the "Count and Take Out" falls on the
uncolored peg the puzzle must be begun anew.

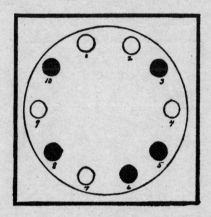

Solution for the Ten Colored Pegs Circle Puzzle

Starting at number 2 peg on diagram, and counting to 11 will
eliminate all of the uncolored pegs.

Starting at number 10 peg on diagram and counting to 29
will eliminate all of the colored pegs.

Do not give the numbers used, rather state the puzzle in the
following manner:—to remove the uncolored pegs use a number
from 1 to 15, and to remove the colored pegs use a number from
15 to 30. In this way the puzzle will not be as easily solved.

Clock Puzzle

Materials and method of constructing clock puzzle:

Use a board four inches square. On it draw a circle
three inches in diameter. Subdivide the circle into

twelve equal parts. At points marked draw circles ½ inch in diameter. Within the circles as per diagram print Roman numerals from one to twelve. Make ten pieces of wire about six inches long.

Puzzle: Using the pieces of wire to indicate knife cuts, divide the clock into four pie-shaped pieces so that each piece equals twenty.

Solution shown on diagram.

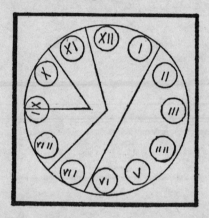

Eight-Peg Circle Puzzle

Materials and method of constructing the eight peg circle puzzle.

Use a board four inches square. Draw a three inch circle on it. Subdivide the circle into eight equal parts. At center of circle and at points marked off drill nine ¼ inch holes. After sand papering the board draw the puzzle design on the board. This can be done with pencil or paint. Make eight ¼ by 1 inch pegs by ½ inch. Glue paper numbers to tops of pegs or if you prefer, carve the numbers on one tip of peg. Fill carving with a colored wood filler; when dry varnish or stain the pegs. Place the eight pegs on board as per diagram. If you prefer, use the same pegs used in the twelve colored peg puzzle, except that the alphabet will be used in place of numbers.

Puzzle: By moving seven of the pegs, rearrange the numbered pegs into a consecutive order around the circle, keeping one of the pegs in the same position at all times.

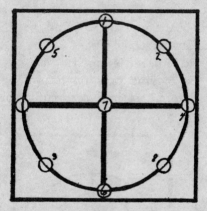

Solution for the Eight Peg Circle Puzzle

(DO NOT MOVE THE PEG NUMBER 5.)

MOVE PEGS NUMBERED:

7-6-3-7-6-1-2-4-1-3-8-1-3-2-4-3-2
Solved in 17 moves

Nine Peg Three Circle Puzzle

Materials and method of constructing nine peg puzzle.

Use a board four inches square. On it draw one three inch circle, one two inch circle, and one one inch circle. Subdivide the three circles into three equal parts. At points indicated on diagram drill ¼ inch holes; connect these holes as per diagram. This can be done with pencil lines. Make nine ¼ inch by 1 inch wood pegs. To one tip of three wood pegs, glue three number one's, to three more glue three number two's, to the remaining three pegs three number three's. If you plan on making use of this puzzle in connection with your work it is advisable to carve the numbers into peg tops, and then filling the carved notches with colored wood filler, plastic wood or some such material. When this is complete varnish the board and you will find that the heavy pencilled circular and straight lines will be very permanent. Set up puzzle as per diagram.

Puzzle: By moving pegs along any one channel rearrange the numbers into consecutive order, that is, 1-2-3-.

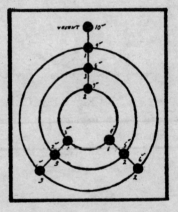

Solution for the Nine Peg Three Circle Puzzle

MOVE PEG NUMBERED (READ DOWN):

9 to 10	2 to 5	8 to 7
6 to 9	3 to 2	9 to 8
5 to 6	7 to 3	10 to 9

Solved in 9 moves

Ten Colored Peg Circle Puzzle

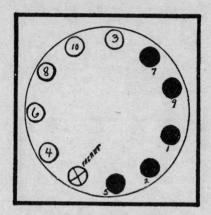

Materials and method of constructing the ten peg circle puzzle.

Use a board four inches square. On it draw a three inch circle. Subdivide the circle into eleven equal parts. At points marked, drill ¼ inch holes. Make ten ¼ inch by 1 inch pegs. To one tip of pegs glue or carve out numbers from one to ten. Color five pegs and leave five pegs uncolored. Set up puzzle as per diagram. Make pegs similar to the twelve peg line puzzle or use the pegs already made, then substitute the alphabet in place of the numbers.

Puzzle: By moving pegs, rearrange the numbers consecutively, that is, 1-2-3-4-5-6-7-8-9-10. Uncolored pegs move or jump in clockwise manner, that is, to right and only over a colored peg. The colored pegs move or jump in a counter clockwise manner and only over an uncolored peg.

Solution for the Ten Colored Peg Circle Puzzle

MOVE PEG NUMBERED:

5-4-6-5-2-1-4-6-8-10-5-2-1
9-7-4-6-8-10-3-5-4-6-8-10-1

Solved in 26 moves

Eleven Peg Circle Puzzle

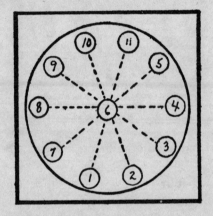

Materials and method of constructing the eleven peg circle puzzle.

Use a board four inches square. On it draw a three inch circle. Subdivide this circle into ten equal parts. At center and at points marked, drill ¼ inch holes. Make eleven wooden pegs, ¼ by 1 inch in length. On one end of the peg glue paper numbers or carve numbers from one to eleven.

Puzzle: Place the eleven pegs in such a position so that any three numbers in a straight line will add up to 18.

Solution shown on diagram.

Twelve Ring Circle Puzzle

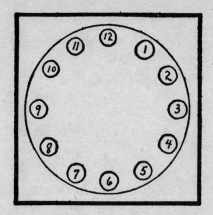

Materials and method of constructing twelve ring circle puzzle.

Use a board four inches square. On it draw a three inch circle. Subdivide the circle into twelve equal parts. At points marked, place one inch wire brads. On each wire brad lace a ¼ inch washer.

Puzzle: Rearrange the twelve washers into six piles, with two washers on each pile by jumping over two washers in any direction.

Solution for the Twelve Ring Circle Puzzle
MOVE RING NUMBERED (READ DOWN):

12 to nail 3
7 to nail 4
10 to nail 6
8 to nail 1
9 to nail 5
11 to nail 2

Solved in 6 moves

Twelve Peg Circle Puzzle

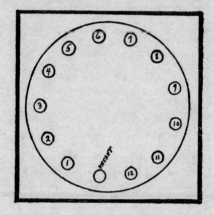

Materials and method of constructing the twelve peg circle puzzle.

Use a board six inches square. On it draw a five inch circle. Subdivide this circle into thirteen equal parts. At points marked off, drill ¼ inch holes. Make twelve pegs ¼ inch by 1 inch long. Glue numbers from one to twelve or carve out the numbers on the tops of pegs. Fill in the carved notches with wood filler or other plastic compound. Set up puzzle as shown on diagram.

Puzzle: By moving peg in either direction to an empty hole, or jumping over a peg reverse the numbers, that is 12 to 1, 11 to 2, etc.

Solution for the Twelve Peg Circle Puzzle

MOVE PEG NUMBERED:

12-1-3-2-12-11-1-3-2-5-7
9-10-8-6-4-3-2-12-11-2-1-2

Solved in 23 moves

Twelve Colored and Numbered Peg Circle Puzzle

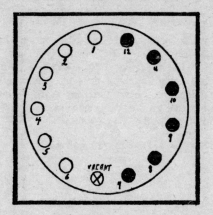

Materials and method of constructing the twelve peg puzzle.

Use a board six inches square. On it draw a five inch circle. With a protractor subdivide the circle into thirteen equal parts. At points marked off drill ¼ inch holes. Make twelve pegs ¼ inch by 1 inch long. Color six of the pegs, stain or leave the other six in their natural color. Glue or carve numbers from one to twelve on the top of pegs. Set up puzzle as per diagram.

Puzzle: By moving peg into an empty hole or by jumping over a peg, reverse the colors in clockwise manner, so that number one peg be in the position of number twelve peg and number two be in the position of number eleven peg, and so on. Colored pegs must move in one direction, the uncolored in opposite direction.

Solution for the Twelve Colored and Numbered Peg Circle Puzzle

MOVE PEG NUMBERED:

6-7-8-6-5-4-7-8-9-10-6-5-4-3-2-7-8-9-10-11. Now move the following pegs five times over—6-5-4-3-2-1. Now that you have not moved the pegs more or less than five times, move peg numbered 6-5-4-3-2-12. Now move the following pegs five times over:—7-8-9-10-11-12. If you have not moved the pegs more or less than five times you will arrive at the solution by moving 7-8-9-10-1-6-5-4-3-2-12-7-8-9-10-11-6-5-4-3-2-8-9-10-11-4-3-2-10-11-2.

Solved in 118 moves

Thirteen Peg Circle Puzzle

Materials and method of constructing the thirteen peg circle puzzle.

Use a board six inches square. On it draw a five inch circle. Subdivide this circle into thirteen parts. Drill ¼ inch holes at points marked off. Make thirteen ¼ inch by 1 inch pegs. Color one of the pegs, leave the other twelve uncolored, set up puzzle as per diagram.

Puzzle: By playing the game of "Count and Take Out" what number and at what peg will count start so that all uncolored pegs are eliminated, leaving the colored peg the last peg on the board? To make puzzle less difficult state it in the following manner: what number from one to twenty-five will eliminate, etc.? As for instance if you choose number 15, starting at number 1 peg, or colored peg you would remove number 2 peg, which is the fifteenth peg. A peg removed is not counted.

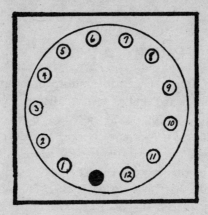

Solution for the Thirteen Peg Circle Puzzle

Start at peg number 6 and count to 13, removing peg number 5. Start the next count at number 6 peg and so on until all but the colored peg remain.

CHECKER BOARD PUZZLES

The game of checkers is, no doubt, the most popular of two-handed board games so that directions concerning the making of this puzzle need not be given. However, I would advise that the checker board be made so that round wooden pegs are used in place of checkers. The reason for this request is that a peg board has more puzzle appeal, than an ordinary checker board. This because a peg placed in position has more permanency and furthermore a peg board need not be as large in size. I do advise that the puzzles be large enough so that they be easier to handle, but you will find that a pocket size peg board can be carried along and played at any time or any place, whereas if you make them large and bulky the place of usage is limited. Don't permit my whims and fancies about size and construction of the board to interfere with your puzzling interests. An ordinary checker board will serve the purpose.

Eight Pegs on Checkerboard Puzzle

Problem: Place eight pegs on checker board in such positions so that no two are in the same straight line, horizontally, vertically or diagonally.

The solution is shown on diagram. Because other solutions are possible, it is advisable to keep a record of them.

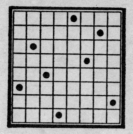

Sixteen Pegs on Checker Board Puzzle

Problem: Place sixteen pegs on a checker board so that two checkers and only two, are in the same straight line, vertically, horizontally and diagonally.

The solution is indicated on the diagram. Because other solutions are possible, it is advisable to keep a record of the positions possible.

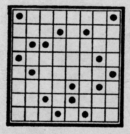

Sixteen Pegs Checker Board Puzzle

Using only three rows of a checker board, place pegs as indicated on diagram. Use fifteen white pegs and one black peg, and this black peg to be (as per diagram) the number 9 peg.

Problem: By jumping in a straight line but not diagonally, and removing peg jumped over, remove the fifteen white pegs.

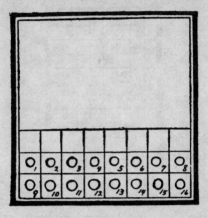

Solution for the Sixteen Pegs Checker Board Puzzle

MOVE PEGS NUMBERED (READ DOWN):

Jump	11	over	3	remove	3
"	1	"	2	"	2
"	9	"	10	"	10
"	15	"	7	"	7
"	16	"	8	"	8
"	16	"	15	"	15
"	13	"	5	"	5
"	9	"	12	"	12

Jump	16	over	13	remove	13
"	14	"	6	"	6
"	11	"	16	"	16
"	14	"	11	"	11
"	14	"	4	"	4
"	9	"	14	"	14
"	9	"	1	"	1

Solved in 15 moves

"Checkers" Checker Board Puzzle

Place pegs on board as in checker game, except that thirty-two pegs are used. Sixteen black pegs and sixteen white pegs and these being on opposite sides of the board as indicated on diagram.

Problem: By jumping pegs in a straight line, and removing peg jumped, remove all but two pegs and these two must be of the same color.

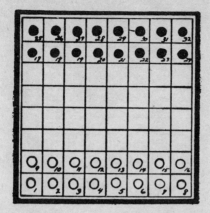

Solution for the "Checkers" Checker Board Puzzle

MOVE PEGS NUMBERED (READ DOWN):

Jump	7 over 15 remove 15	Jump	32 over 24 remove 24
"	8 " 16 " 16	"	32 " 31 " 31
"	8 " 7 " 7	"	26 " 18 " 18
"	2 " 10 " 10	"	25 " 17 " 17
"	1 " 9 " 9	"	25 " 26 " 26
"	1 " 2 " 2	"	22 " 32 " 32
"	5 " 13 " 13	"	14 " 22 " 22
"	3 " 4 " 4	"	29 " 21 " 21
"	6 " 3 " 3	"	14 " 29 " 29
"	11 " 1 " 1	"	27 " 28 " 28
"	14 " 8 " 8	"	30 " 27 " 27
"	6 " 12 " 12	"	25 " 14 " 14
"	5 " 6 " 6	"	30 " 20 " 20
"	5 " 11 " 11	"	25 " 30 " 30
"	31 " 23 " 23	"	25 " 5 " 5

Solved in 30 moves with two black checkers on board

Checker Board Solitaire Puzzle

The Solitaire Puzzle is the most difficult of checker board puzzles, but I am not furnishing a solution for it because it is a good way to put an end to checker board puzzles.

Here it is: Place pegs as per diagram on all of the outer checker spaces, now play as in checkers, removing the pegs jumped on diagonal moves. Play for the least number of pegs on the board. To have one peg on board is a very difficult feat. Try it and you will agree that it is the puzzle of puzzles.

CHECKER BOARD STRING
PUZZLES

The checker board string puzzle is exceptionally good for the chess minded individual because all chess players spend their leisure moments playing with either the Rooks Tour, Knights Tour and other such chess moves. But one need not be a chess enthusiast to try his or her skill with this puzzle. The puzzle does not require elaborate equipment nor does it demand any special skills. The oldster enjoys this puzzle as much as does the youngster. All one needs to have to play it is a piece of string, and a checker board in which nails and screws replace the usual checker squares. The board can be made out of apple box wood. However, it is advisable to use wood that is at least ½ inch to 1 inch in thickness. If wood of such size is used the nails can be imbedded to give them more firmness. Do not use a board smaller than one foot square. If you do you will find it difficult to handle. On the board draw a checker board design. In the center of each of the 64 squares place either 1 inch nails or 1 inch screws. It is advisable to use 32 nails and 32 screws so that the checker board effect is retained.

When the nails and screws are placed, carve or paint the squares for each of the five string puzzles in this book.

When your puzzle board is constructed, type the puzzle problem as stated in directions. Glue these directions onto back of board and then with piece of string proceed to solve the puzzles.

15 Line Puzzle

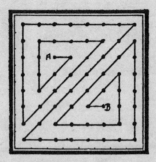

Go from A to B, touching all of the pegs, in 15 consecutive straight lines, either horizontal, vertical or diagonal. No line may cross another.

Solution shown on diagram.

17 Line Puzzle

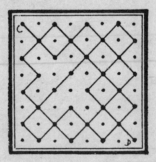

Using only the nails as points of connecting lines, go from point C to D in 17 consecutive straight lines. In this puzzle the lines may cross each other.

Solution shown on diagram.

15 Line Puzzle

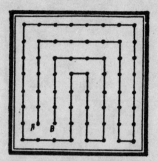

Go from A to B, touching all of the pegs, in 15 consecutive straight lines. Diagonal lines prohibited. No line may cross another line.

Solution shown on diagram.

21 Line Puzzle

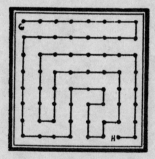

Go from G to H, touching all of the pegs, in 21 consecutive straight lines. Diagonal lines are prohibited Another rule or objective is occasionally added to the problem and that is—the tenth line must end at peg H. However, this is just another version and need not be added.

Solution shown on diagram.

12 Line Puzzle

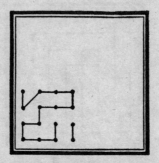

Using only 16 nail pegs, go from J to K, touching all of the pegs, in 12 consecutive straight lines. Use horizontal, vertical or diagonal lines. No line may cross another line.

Solution shown on diagram.

CHINESE CHESS BOARD

A great many Chinese chess boards are now being stored in attics and basements, gathering dust and cobwebs. So why not resurrect the one that you have and thereon try one of the following puzzles?

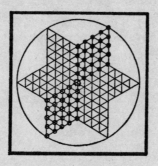

Place pegs on board as per diagram. The puzzle would be to reverse the colored pegs, by moving into an empty hole or by jumping over one peg. This chess puzzle is similar to the 33 peg puzzle except that 48 pegs are used, that is 24 red pegs and 24 black pegs.

#2.

When you have mastered the number one puzzle, place a peg in every hole except the center hole. The puzzle would be to reverse the colors, by moving into an empty hole or by jumping over one peg. The material requirements are six sets of colored pegs, with either a colored chess board or a board upon which marks designating direction of movement can be made.

#3.

When number two has been solved, replace the pegs on board in all holes except the center hole. The puzzle now would be to remove all pegs except one and that one to be in center of board. To arrive at that solution is very difficult so don't attempt it on the first trial; rather try to remove all pegs except one peg and that peg to be anywhere on the board.

STRING PUZZLES

The title of this group of puzzles is misleading in that most of the puzzles are made of leather lacing. However, the originators of this type of puzzle used string or cord when devising or creating what today are called string puzzles. Due to the availability and durability of leather lacings, string is seldom used for this group of puzzles. Other well known names for these puzzles are "Sailors Puzzles," and "Tailors Puzzles." This because in the annals of antiquity the followers of those two trades or pursuits are credited with being the originators and creators of rope and string tricks and puzzles.

A chance statement ought not to be taken into consideration as proof of a law or fact but you will find that when a string puzzler gets tangled into a knot or knots and a solution is nigh onto impossible, he invariably makes a comment to the effect that a sailor of old must have created the puzzle, or that a tailor devised it in his spare time or hectic moments.

The string puzzles are dandy pocket puzzles and especially good for convalescents. It is a type of puzzle that is very popular yet very discouraging so don't expect an immediate 100% return for your labors in making it.

To construct the puzzle use leather lacing as a substitute for string. The lacings can be purchased in any Leather Goods Store, Department Store and in most 5¢ and 10¢ stores. For the block part of puzzle, use either plywood, leather or linoleum.

Two Balls and Cord Puzzle

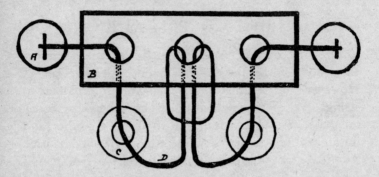

Puzzle: Without untying the knots on both ends, get the two beads or washers on the same side.

Materials used for this puzzle:

One oblong 1½ by 6 inches strip of wood, linoleum, cardboard or metal.

Four large metal washers, buttons or beads.

One piece of string, thin leather lacing or fishing cord at least two feet long. The leather lacing is preferred because it can be handled easier than string.

To construct puzzle: Into the wood block drill three ½ inch holes, equal distances apart. Tie a button, bead, or washer to one end of the string. Take the free end and put it from the top side through the left hole; next thread a washer or bead onto the string. From bottom side put string through center hole. Now thread a washer or bead onto string. Next from bottom side put free end of string through right hole. Tie a washer or button onto free end. Puzzle is now assembled. Consult diagram for assistance in assembling the puzzle.

Solution for the Two Balls and Cord Puzzle

Pull the center loop, down, put one of the beads or washers through it. Now put the loop through the hole on the side where bead was passed through loop. When this has been done pull the loop back to center. Do the same with the other side. Now pull the loop through center hole and you'll find that the beads will now be on the same side.

Needle Puzzle

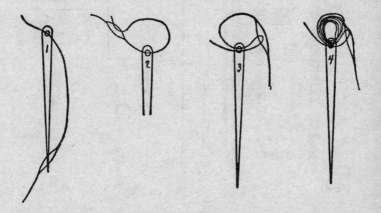

This is not what some puzzlers call a puzzle, but the layman calls it a "Needle Puzzle," therefore, it is included in this group of puzzles; however, it is primarily a stunt or trick.

Materials used for this puzzle: One needle and one spool of thread.

Puzzle: How was needle threaded?

To construct puzzle: Thread a needle, about six inches from end of the thread, twist thread and you'll find that a loop will be formed. Now put the needle through this loop and then pull loop through needle hole. The more often you pull this loop through needle hole, the more threads the needle will contain. When you have the needle fully threaded cut the loops formed and show it to your friends with this as the puzzle problem: How was this needle threaded?

Chinese Ladder Puzzle

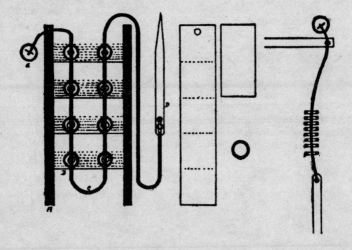

Materials used for this puzzle: Two pieces of cigar box wood, 1 inch by 6 inches long. Four pieces of cigar box wood, 1 inch by 2 inches. Nine ½ inch metal washers. One large needle. Three feet of fishing cord. Wire brads or small nails.

To construct puzzle: Mark off lines 1 inch apart on the two long pieces of wood. Drill a ¼ inch hole into the top end of one of the long pieces of wood. Drill two ⅛ inch holes into each of the four rungs or shelves. Make these holes equidistance apart. Do not drill holes into each board separately. If a vise or clamp is handy put the four 2 inch pieces of wood into it and drill the four holes at one time. When this is complete use ½ inch wire brads to construct a miniature bookcase out of the two long and four small pieces of wood. Shellac or varnish the ladder and let dry.

To one end of the three foot cord attach a metal washer which must be larger than the hole in the top of the 6 inch piece of wood. To the other end attach a large needle.

To assemble puzzle: Put needle into hole at top of bookcase or ladder then thread a washer onto string; then through the ladder rung; next a washer, through rung; then a washer, then through rung. From bottom come through holes on the right through rung, through washer; through rung, through washer; through rung, through washer; through rung, through washer. Puzzle is now assembled.

Consult diagram for assistance in assembling puzzle.

Puzzle: Remove the washers and string from the ladder rungs but not from the ladder upright or ladder leg, having all washers threaded on the string as per diagram.

Solution for the Chinese Ladder Puzzle

If the directions are followed the puzzle is not difficult so proceed in the following manner. Wind a portion of the string around the lower right ladder leg. Two loops are sufficient. When doing this make certain that you have at least two feet of cord or string to puzzle with. Do not draw the cord in the ladder taut, allow a little play in the string. Now put the needle through rung holes and washers going from the right bottom rung, call it number 4 rung to number one rung, then down on left side, through 1 to 4 rung. But only through rungs not through washers.

The second step is to make a loop with string on lower left

ladder leg. When this has been done thread the washers. Do not thread the ladder rungs. Start on bottom left side working to top, then down on right side to bottom.

The third step is to remove the string loops from the ladder legs.

When the loops have been removed pull on the needle end of the string. If the directions were followed, the washers should now be threaded on the string as per diagram.

One Ball and String Puzzle

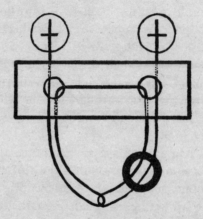

Materials used for this puzzle: One oblong strip of wood 1½ inches wide by 5 inches long. One thin leather lacing, string or fish line cord about two feet long One wood ball or metal washer. Two large buttons or washers.

To construct puzzle: Drill two ½ inch holes into the oblong strip of wood. Tie a button to one end of lacing. Take the free end and from the bottom side pass it through the hole on the right. Thread the ball or washer onto string. Make a loop and re-thread the ball from bottom side; pass free end through hole on right, to hole on left, through loop of ball and back through left hole. Puzzle is now assembled.

Consult diagram for assistance in assembling puzzle.

Puzzle: Without untying the button ends, remove the ball from the lacing.

Solution for the One Ball and String Puzzle

Pull loop coming out of ball through hole at left, over washer tied to lacing and pull back. Ball can now be removed.

Key Puzzle

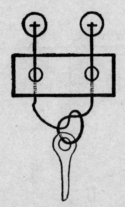

Puzzle: Without removing the buttons, release the knot about the key. The key will then be on the string but without a knot.

Materials used for this puzzle: One oblong strip of wood or leather whose size is at least 4 inches by 1½ inches by ¼ inch in thickness. One key. One piece of thin leather lacing, fish cord, or smooth twine, at least 18 inches in length. Two large washers or large buttons.

To construct the puzzle:

Drill two ½ inch holes into the strip of wood or thick leather. Tie a button or washer onto one end of the string. Put the untied end through one of the holes; next tie an over-hand knot into the key. Put end of string through other hole and to the end tie the second washer or button. Consult diagram for assistance in assembling puzzle.

Solution for the Key Puzzle

Pull one of the loops through the right hole in block, put it over the button and then pull it back through the hole. If directions were followed the knot will have disappeared. To replace knot, reverse the action.

Two pieces of Leather and Lacing Puzzle

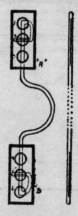

Puzzle: Remove leather lacing from the two thick leather strips or plywood blocks.

Materials used to make this puzzle: Two pieces of leather about ¼ inch thick, or pieces of plywood, heavy linoleum, or heavy cardboard. The two pieces of leather should be 2 inches long and 1¼ inches wide. One leather lacing at least ¼ inch wide, and 18 inches long. The lacing can be purchased in any leather goods store.

To construct the puzzle: Drill three holes ½ inch in diameter into the two leather or plywood pieces. About one half inch from ends of lacing cut a slit about 2½ inches in length.

· To assemble puzzle: Take one end of the lacing and put it from the bottom side through hole #2 in diagram. Take the other end and put it from the bottom side through hole #1, then through the slit in the lacing, then through hole #3 and out through the bottom side. Take the free end of the lacing and from the bottom side put it through hole #4, then through hole #6, then from bottom side through hole #5. Now take the free end and put it from the top side through hole #4. Pull it through so that the slot is clear from the block. Now put block "A" through the slit in the lacing and then pull the slit end back through hole #4 and you'll find that "B" will be assembled as is block "A."

Consult diagram for assistance in assembling this puzzle.

To work puzzle proceed as in the directions.

Leather and String Puzzle

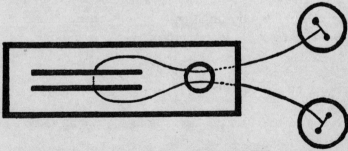

Puzzle: Remove string from leather strip.

Materials required for this puzzle: 1 piece of soft thin

leather or piece of cloth, at least 5 inches long by 1½ inches wide; 1 piece of thin leather lacing, fishing cord, or ordinary string; 2 large washers, rings or buttons.

To construct puzzle proceed in the following manner: Draw a circle on the piece of leather as per diagram. Then using a sharp knife with a narrow edged blade cut out the circle. Make this hole at least ½ inch in diameter. When you have the hole made, draw two lines as per diagram, making the distance between the lines slightly less than the diameter of the circle. It is also advisable to cut out a very narrow piece where the slits are made. This will help to deceive the puzzler. Make these slits at least 2 inches in length.

Take a piece of string at least 1 foot in length and to the ends of each tie a washer, ring or button. The buttons or washers must be larger than the hole in the leather or cloth strip.

To assemble puzzle: Take hold of the loose strip of leather and push it through the round hole on opposite end. Put one of the buttons attached to the string through this strip. Pull back the leather strip. Center your string and the puzzle is assembled. Consult diagram for assistance in assembling this puzzle.

To remove the string, proceed as in assembling.

Block and String Puzzle

Puzzle: Remove the lacing from the two-holed board without untying the lacing.

Materials used for this puzzle: One piece of thick or heavy leather, plywood, linoleum or cardboard, 1½ inches wide by 4 inches long. One piece of fishing cord, thin leather lacing or string. One large button.

To construct and assemble the puzzle: Drill two holes ½ inch in diameter into the wood block. Put the two ends of the string through the button holes and tie them into a knot. The button must be larger than the holes in the board. Take the loop of the cord and from the bottom side put it through hole number 1. Now take the loop, pass it through hole number 2. Next take loop and

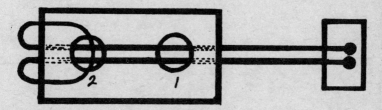

pass it through hole number 1, and over button. Now pull the loop back to hole number 2 and you will find that the puzzle is assembled.

Consult diagram for assistance in assembling the puzzle.

SOLUTION: Proceed as in assembling.

Two Holed Block and String Puzzle

Puzzle: Remove leather lacing from the two blocks without untying loops.

Materials used for this puzzle: Two pieces of ¼ inch leather, plywood, metal or heavy cardboard, 1¼ inches by 3 inches. One leather lacing at least two feet long.

To construct and assemble the puzzle: Drill two

holes, ½ inch in diameter, into each of the two pieces
of leather. Glue or wire a two inch loop onto each end
of the lacing. Put one end of the lacing from the bottom through hole number 1 in leather block, then
through hole number 2. Now bring loop through hole

number 1 and pass leather lacing through it; then pull
the loop back through hole number 1. Do the same
with the other two holed leather block.

Consult diagram for assistance in assembling puzzle.

To remove leather lacing reverse the assembly directions.

Leather and Two String Puzzle

Puzzle: Remove the two lacings from the leather
strip.

Materials used for this puzzle: One piece of thin
leather or cloth, 1½ inches wide by 5 inches long. Four
large washers or buttons. These must be larger than the

holes in the leather. Two thin leather lacings, string or fishing cord each 10 inches long.

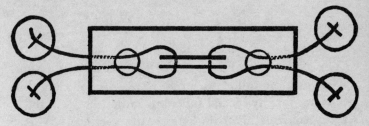

To construct and assemble the puzzle: Cut two ½ inch holes into the piece of leather or cloth. Now cut two slits about two inches long into the thin leather piece. The slit in the leather must not be wider than the diameter of the holes. Tie buttons or washers onto ends of the leather lacings. Now put a flap through left hole; through this loop pass one of the lacings with buttons attached. Pull the flap back. Do the same with the right side.

Consult diagram for assistance in assembling puzzle.

GLASS TOPPED BOX
PUZZLES

The glass topped box puzzle is English in origin and has its greatest following in England. Its solution depends not on any special skills but rather on one's ability to control his own muscular reactions. When working on this type of puzzle, the puzzler has two things to control, one the puzzle itself and the other his own anxiety to help the puzzle along. As for instance the balancing puzzle requires a high degree of patience control, therefore, don't attempt to solve it when your nerves are on edge. Make one and you will agree that it is a nerve wrecker.

The method of constructing this type of puzzle is as follows: Use either cigar box or apple box wood. For the square box puzzles cut a piece of wood nine inches square (or three inches by three inches), sand paper both sides and varnish one or both sides of this square piece of wood. When varnish is dry construct the puzzle as per diagram. For the sides of the container use cigar box wood or a heavy grade of cardboard. Make these strips one inch wide. Tack or glue strips to the four edges of the base. Make puzzle designs within container. Cut glass for top of container and with adhesive tape or glued paper, seal the container. When this has been done proceed to work the puzzle.

Shell and Pellet Puzzle

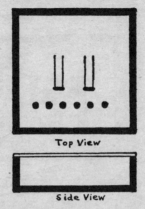

Top View

Side View

Materials and method of constructing shell and pellet puzzle: Make a container nine inches square. Attach two .22 caliber rifle shells or other such size tubes to base of container. The shells can be attached with wire or they can be tacked onto base with a nail through the sealed end. Place six or more $\frac{1}{8}$ inch steel ball bearings into container. Do not use lead shots, because they will not remain perfectly round for any period of time. Seal container with glass cover, and proceed to solve the puzzle whose problem is: Place pellets into bullet shells. You need not use bullet shells but they do add that certain something to make the puzzle more effective.

The Letter "H" Puzzle

Materials and method of constructing the letter "H" puzzle: Make container nine inches square. Within it as per diagram, glue or tack a letter "H" made out of $\frac{1}{8}$ inch wood or heavy cardboard. Subdivide the space

between the arms and color, each of the four spaces
with a different color. Now make four ½ inch wood or
metal discs so that any two will fit between arms of the

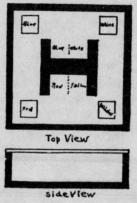

Top View

sideView

letter. Paint the four discs with corresponding colors.
When paint on discs is dry, place them into the container. Seal it with a piece of glass and proceed to solve
the puzzle as follows.

Cover the spots with their respective colored discs.

The Dice Puzzle

Puzzle: By manipulating the container place dice into
holes in numerical order. Another variation is to have
all dice in holes with number one's, two's, three's, or
any other number face up.

Materials and method of constructing the dice puzzle:
Out of cigar box wood make a container nine inches
square by 1 inch high. To the base of the container glue
or tack a ⅜ inch piece of wood, which is two inches
wide and three inches long. Place this piece so that it is
centered in the container, then mark off six squares as

per diagram. At the six center points of the squares drill
⅜ inch holes. With a sharp, thin pointed knife convert
the round holes into square holes. To make holes accurate and exact in size use a narrow file to remove any
rough edges. Make holes large enough for the dice to
slide through the holes. With a pencil, mark holes as

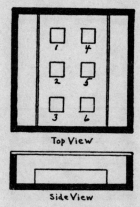

Top View

Side View

per diagram. Varnish or shellac container. When dry,
place the six dice into container. Cover container with
glass and seal it with adhesive tape or glued paper. Do
not use the regulation size dice; the ⅜ inch dice are the
best size to use. This because dice of this size are easier
to manipulate, in that if the wrong side of dice turns up,
the snapping of the thumb on bottom side of box will
remove the dice out of wrong hole.

Five Babes and Nursemaid Puzzle

Puzzle: By manipulating the container, place the
"Five Babes" into their beds with nurse overlooking
them.

This is a puzzle that is very entertaining and fun to

work. If you have a two year old youngster near you, you had better not leave the puzzle lying around because if you do you'll be replacing the pellets rather often, in that youngsters are fascinated by the tumbling of the pellets; of course even grown ups enjoy playing with this puzzle, but usually they do not handle it as roughly.

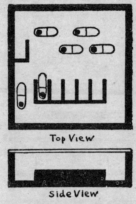

Top View

Side View

Materials and methods of constructing the five babes and nursemaid puzzle: Out of cigar box wood make a container nine inches square. Within it construct five stalls to represent beds with back attached, and one stall attached to side of box. Make these stalls out of ¼ inch pieces of wood. Glue or tack these strips to base of box. On your way home from office or shop stop in at the neighborhood drug store and purchase six (plus a few extra) drug capsules. Within each capsule place a steel or lead pellet and seal capsules with a bit of glue. If you want to make the puzzle very difficult, color each capsule and color stall with corresponding color. When construction is complete, seal the puzzle with a piece of glass and adhesive tape.

The Cup and Pellets Puzzle

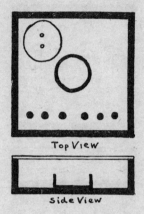

Top View

Side View

Puzzle: By manipulating container, place the steel pellets into cup, and then cover cup with button.

This puzzle demands considerable patience and manipulative skill, but if time hangs heavy on your hands you will find it rather easy to solve.

Materials and method of constructing the cup and pellets puzzle: Out of cigar box wood make a container nine inches square. In the center of this place the top of a catsup bottle whose sides have been cut down so that it is at least ⅜ inch in depth. Attach this metal cup with either tack or small screw. When this is attached, place six steel pellets into container. Do not use lead pellets because they do not remain round for very long. Then seek until you find a stray overcoat button and when found, appropriated, or removed from that old overcoat, place it into container. Seal container with glass and adhesive tape.

The Nail and Eyelets Puzzle

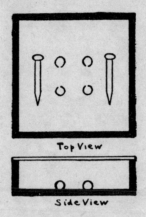

Top View

Side View

Puzzle: By manipulating box, place the nails into the eyelets. They can be placed in either manner, heads of nails on one end or a head on each end.

Materials and methods of constructing the nail and eyelets puzzle: Out of cigar box wood make a container nine inches square. Into the base of container screw four ⅜ inch eyelets, at least ¾ inch apart, or if you'd rather you may use four ¼ inch wire staples. Next take two 1 inch nails, file or sandpaper the ends so that they have a needle point, and so that any rough edges be removed. Place the nails into container and seal it with glass and adhesive tape.

Nine Pegs and Eight Rings Puzzle

Puzzle: By manipulating container place a colored ring on its respective colored peg. When you feel that you are a master of ringing the pegs, place as many of the rings on the center peg as is possible.

Material and method of constructing the nine pegs
and rings puzzle: Out of cigar box wood make a container nine inches square. On the base of container
draw a 2 inch circle. Divide this circle into eight equal
parts. At points marked off, place ⅛ inch by ½ inch
wooden pegs. Color each peg differently. Purchase eight

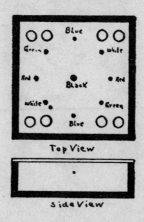

Top View

side View

½ inch celluloid curtain tie back holder rings from any
five and ten cent store or notions store. Color each ring
with corresponding colors. When the rings are dry,
place them into the container. Cover the container with
glass and seal it with adhesive tape or glued paper.

Six Bars in Trap Puzzle

Puzzle: By manipulating container, arrange bars into
their respective traps.

Materials and method of constructing the six bar
puzzle: Out of cigar box wood make a container three
inches by three inches by one inch in height. Make a

trap as per diagram out of ⅛ inch cardboard or wood.
Glue or tack this trap to base of box. Make six ⅛ inch
round metal bars according to trap sizes. Do not make
these out of wood because wood of such size does not

Top View

Side View

roll easily. Nails are very satisfactory. Cut them to size
and then sandpaper ends. Place metal bars into container. Seal it with glass and adhesive tape.

The Ball Balancing Puzzle

Puzzle: By manipulating container, balance the ball
bearing on the balance beam.

Materials and method of constructing the balancing
puzzle: Out of cigar box wood make a container 2 inches
wide by 5 inches long by 1 inch high. Out of tin or
other thin metal construct a flat bottomed "U" shaped
figure 2½ inches long by ½ inch wide. Cut the ends
of the scoop as per diagram. Through the center of the
scoop arms drill a hole whose size will depend upon

the size of the beam bar to be used. A nail is very satisfactory as a beam bar. Through the center of the scoop
bottom drill a hole slightly smaller than the ⅜ inch
steel ball bearing to be used. Attach the metal balance

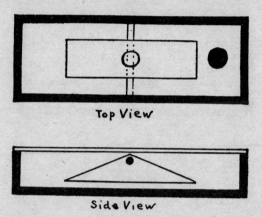

Top View

Side View

to the sides of the container so that it be at least ¼
inch above base of container. Place ⅜ inch ball bearing
into container, cover container with glass, and seal with
adhesive tape or glued paper strips.

The Mercury Bowling Puzzle

Puzzle: By manipulating the container place a bit of
mercury into each of the ten holes.

Materials and method of constructing the bowling
puzzle: Out of cigar box wood make a container 2 inches
wide by 5 inches long. To represent a bowling alley,
glue or tack a ⅛ inch piece of wood, 1 inch wide by
5 inches long to the bottom of container. On one end
of the bowling alley drill ten holes; do not make them

deeper than mere drill points. If you make them very deep you will have to use a considerable amount of mercury. Now place a piece of mercury into the container. Amount of mercury used depends upon size of holes

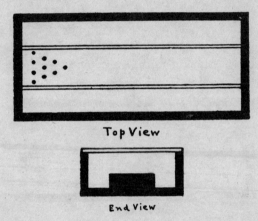

Top View

End View

drilled. Cover container with glass and seal with adhesive tape. When sealing this puzzle keep in mind that if puzzle is not sealed tightly the mercury will be lost.

Another variation is to use ten steel pellets instead of the mercury.

SIX PIECE BURR PUZZLE

I have over a thousand mechanical and manipulative puzzles in my collection and very often I am asked what one puzzle I enjoy the most. True it is some puzzles are very interesting and entertaining, yet of them all, I prefer the six piece burr or Jack puzzle. It is the simplest yet most difficult of puzzles. There are but six pieces to work with and the design is easy to visualize. It is not a complex puzzle; and it is disassembled in a hurry but not assembled as hurriedly. It is the kind of puzzle that is forever puzzling.

Within this portion of the book are recorded seventy-three different combinations by using thirty-eight different burrs. This collection in itself is a prize collection and to my knowledge it is the most complete of the burr puzzle combinations. The combinations have been collected the world over by correspondence, travel and research into ancient books of magic, tricks, games and puzzles. No doubt there are a few more to be added and some day that number of combinations will be enlarged. If you have one that is not included do drop me a card. I do not profess to be able to work each and every one on the spur of the moment but each and every combination herein recorded has been assembled. I am in no position to say which is the most difficult, but I assure you that many an hour was spent in attempting to verify a new combination.

It is not absolutely necessary to make the four hundred and thirty-two pieces, but if you want a complete collection it is advisable to do so. If you do that, you can mark each piece so that your second assembly will be easier and more rapid.

The tools required for this puzzle are a saw and a knife. Of course it is advisable to have a square and file, but they are not necessary. If you are a wood working hobbyist and have a band saw and a jig-saw, you will discover that making the pieces will be very simple. However, do make a jig and you'll spend less time making the pieces and they will be more accurate.

The majority of these puzzles are assembled "piece meal," that is one piece follows another. Some of the combinations especially those that do not have the number "1" or "locking piece" are very difficult because they are assembled in either pairs of two, three, or four. By that is meant that you assemble three pieces and then slide the two sections of three pieces together. So don't try to solve the difficult ones first, if you do you will be discouraged in a hurry. Endeavor to solve the combinations with the number one or locking piece before attempting the difficult combinations.

By having so many different combinations of the same puzzle, you can have loads of fun, not only fun of your own, but you can also use this puzzle to entertain your friends when you don't want to spend the night just playing cards. Most of these combinations are solid assemblies, a few are not. If you want to try a new party idea, why not give each of the party attendants one set of pieces and then at a designated time have all of them endeavor to assemble the puzzle given them.

For the recreational leader this puzzle is "tops" because a new puzzle can be used daily. It is also a dandy contest idea.

The Six Piece Burr Puzzle

The six piece burr or "Jack" puzzle is the most interesting and entertaining puzzle. This is due to the fact that it is the most common of the assembly type of puzzles. The average man in the course of his life has either seen or attempted to solve the burr puzzle, and so you will find that when this puzzle is offered to some one to solve, the response will usually be, "I worked that puzzle years ago." You will also find that it won't demand much encouragement to get another interested in it. They will take it apart in a hurry but woe be it unto them when they try to assemble it. If you are desirous of acquiring a hobby, make a complete set of thirty-eight pieces and then proceed to solve each combination. When you feel that you have mastered a few of them, try them on your freinds. You will find that this puzzle alone will establish your reputation as a puzzle enthusiast.

When making this puzzle make certain that the wood used is perfectly square. To avoid trouble have the lumber made at a mill work shop. The cost of the lumber so made is less than one imagines it to be. Use lumber that is one half inch square. Don't use pieces that are narrower, the half inch are easier to handle and therefore less disturbing to the maker and to the puzzler. Another point to remember—do not use any of the soft woods. The hardwoods are more difficult to work with, but you will find that a puzzle made of hardwood will last longer. When making your pieces don't cut them into three inch lengths. Give yourself an inch to spare. When the puzzle is assembled, place one arm of the burr into a vise and cut the burrs to proper size.

1. Puzzle combination 29 is assembled in the following numerical order.

   4—8—13—12—7—1

2. Puzzle combination 12 is assembled in the following numerical order.

   Piece number 4—4—5—7—7—1

3. Puzzle combination 43 is assembled in the following numerical order.

   Piece number 6—9—7—7—8—1

   Number 1 is the locking piece.

4. Puzzle combination 44 is assembled in the following numerical order.

   Piece number 6—7—12—13—7—1

   when six piece burr is assembled.

   > Numbers 6 and 1 are parallel
   > Numbers 7 and 7 are parallel
   > Numbers 12 and 13 are parallel

   Number 1 is the locking piece.

5. Puzzle combination 46 is assembled in the following numerical order.

   Piece number 6—9—21—22—7—1

   Number 1 is the locking piece.

6. Puzzle combination 49 is assembled in sets of the following numbers.

   Set A consist of numbers 7— 7—10

   Set B consists of numbers 12—13

   Set C or locking piece number 1

   These three sets are assembled by sliding set B and set A together, and then locking these with a number 1 piece.

7. Puzzle combination 50 is assembled in the following numerical order.

   Set A consists of numbers 12— 7—13

Set B consists of numbers 7—11

Set C consists of numbers 1 or locking piece.

Set A and Set B are united by sliding one into the other and locking these five with a number 1 or locking piece.

8. Puzzle combination 63 is assembled in sets of the following numbers.

Set A consists of numbers 2—18—15—14

Set B consists of numbers 32— 7

These two sets are then assembled into one six piece burr puzzle by sliding one set into the other.

9. Puzzle combination 68 is assembled in sets of the following numbers.

Set A consists of numbers 10—12—13

Set B consists of numbers 3— 7—11

These two sets are then assembled into one six piece burr puzzle by sliding one set into the other.

10. Puzzle combination 72 is assembled into sets of the following numbers:

Set A consists of numbers 19—23—27

Set B consists of numbers 10—16—31

These two sets of three pieces are assembled as per diagram. They are united into one six piece burr by sliding one set into the other.

Burr Puzzle

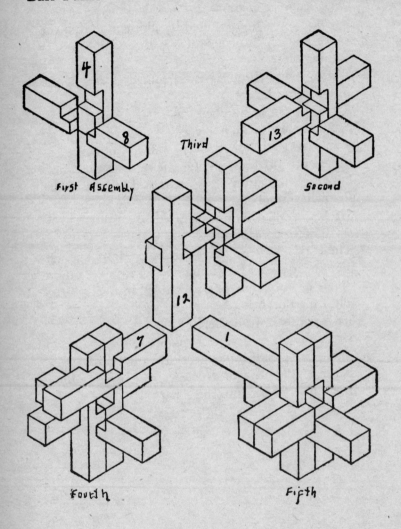

First Assembly

4

8

Third

Second

13

12

7

1

Fourth

Fifth

Six Piece Burr Puzzle

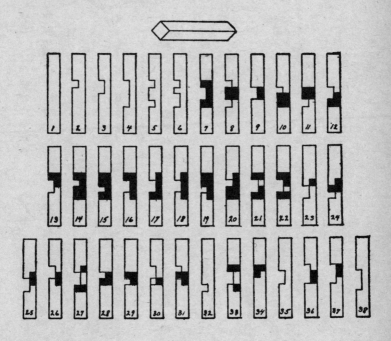

NUMBER 63. The Six Piece Burr Puzzle—73 combinations

Combination number	Numbers—represent piece number					Combination number	Numbers—represent piece number				
1— 1	3	4	7	7	7	38— 1	4	8	12	22	36
2— 1	3	4	7	7	8	39— 1	4	8	13	21	36
3— 1	3	4	7	13	22	40— 1	4	8	21	22	38
4— 1	3	6	7	7	7	41— 1	4	12	13	21	22
5— 1	3	7	7	7	13	42— 1	5	7	7	7	9
6— 1	3	7	7	12	22	43— 1	6	7	7	8	9
7— 1	3	7	7	13	21	44— 1	6	7	7	12	13
8— 1	3	7	7	33	36	45— 1	6	7	7	7	35
9— 1	3	7	7	37	37	46— 1	6	7	9	21	22
10— 1	3	7	21	22	36	47— 1	6	7	21	22	38
11— 1	3	7	21	22	37	48— 1	7	7	8	9	38
12— 1	4	4	5	7	7	49— 1	7	7	10	12	13
13— 1	4	4	4	8	8	50— 1	7	7	11	12	13
14— 1	4	4	6	7	7	51— 1	7	7	12	22	35
15— 1	4	4	6	7	8	52— 1	7	7	12	22	36
16— 1	4	4	6	21	22	53— 1	7	7	13	21	37
17— 1	4	4	7	8	10	54— 1	7	9	21	22	38
18— 1	4	4	7	8	11	55— 1	7	10	13	21	37
19— 1	4	4	8	10	38	56— 1	7	10	21	22	38
20— 1	4	4	10	21	22	57— 1	7	11	12	22	36
21— 1	4	4	11	21	22	58— 1	7	11	21	22	38
22— 1	4	5	7	7	35	59— 1	7	21	22	35	36
23— 1	4	5	7	7	36	60— 1	7	21	22	35	37
24— 1	4	6	6	7	7	61— 1	9	21	22	36	36
25— 1	4	6	7	7	13	62— 1	9	21	22	37	37
26— 1	4	6	7	12	22	63— 2	7	14	15	18	32
27— 1	4	6	7	13	21	64— 3	3	7	7	9	35
28— 1	4	7	7	8	35	65— 3	4	4	5	7	10
29— 1	4	7	8	12	13	66— 3	4	7	7	10	32
30— 1	4	7	7	11	11	67— 3	7	7	10	13	34
31— 1	4	7	7	10	10	68— 3	7	10	11	12	13
32— 1	4	7	10	12	21	69— 7	10	12	11	26	29
33— 1	4	7	11	12	21	70— 7	10	13	11	25	28
34— 1	4	7	10	13	22	71—10	11	12	12	13	13
35— 1	4	7	12	22	36	72—10	16	19	23	27	31
36— 1	4	7	21	35	37	73—11	17	20	24	30	33
37— 1	4	7	21	22	35						

NUMBER OF PIECES REQUIRFD FOR THE 72 DIFFERENT
COMBINATIONS OF THE BURR PUZZLE

Piece number	1—62 pieces			Piece number	21—24 pieces
"	"	2— 1	"	"	"	22—28	"
"	"	3—17	"	"	"	23— 1	"
"	"	4—48	"	"	"	24— 1	"
"	"	5— 5	"	"	"	25— 1	"
"	"	6—14	"	'	"	26— 1	"
"	"	7—94	"	"	"	27— 1	"
"	"	8—14	"	"	"	28— 1	"
"	"	9— 8	"	"	"	29— 1	"
"	"	10—18	"	"	"	30— 1	"
"	"	11—13	"	"	"	31— 1	"
"	"	12—17	"	"	"	32— 2	"
"	"	13—19	"	"	"	33— 1	"
"	"	14— 1	"	"	"	34— 1	"
"	"	15— 1	"	"	"	35— 9	"
"	"	16— 1	"	"	"	36—11	"
"	"	17— 1	"	"	"	37— 9	"
"	"	18— 1	"	"	"	38— 7	"
"	"	19— 1	"			
"	"	20— 1	"			

A total of 438 pieces.

WOOD DESIGN PUZZLES

The puzzles in this group are known by various names but they are essentially assembly puzzles and when assembled they represent some distinct object.

When making this puzzle use an assortment of hard woods. The making of the small pieces out of hard woods is a very difficult task but they do make a more durable and more picturesque puzzle. However if you are interested in the puzzle as a whittling or wood carving project use soft wood.

The cutting of the wood to sizes indicated on the diagram can be done with what are commonly "dream castle tools," that is the electric jig saw, band saw, sander and others found in the Sears and Roebuck model workshop. But a metal saw, file, pocket knife and sharpening stone or a fine grade of sand paper to keep the knife sharp are the most satisfactory tools, because they are the least expensive and most practical.

In the course of my experiences as a summer camp leader, and Milwaukee playground director, I have seen many a man "just whittlin'" and when offered a model of one of the one hundred or more puzzles in this group of puzzles, the whittler seldom if ever spent his free moment "just whittlin'." So that to enjoy these puzzles one need not have an array of tools, all that is necessary is one puzzle to use as a model, plus a boy or oldster with a pocket knife and any kind of wood.

Where possible exact measurements have been recorded. If you make them according to sizes indicated you are "apt" to have an accurate puzzle but woe be it unto you, if you make an error. To avoid this possibility of an error it is advisable that pieces be made in numerical order. Furthermore, make them slightly larger than indicated and then sand paper each piece so as to have a tight fitting puzzle. Do this as you make and assemble each piece. Do not paint or varnish any of the pieces.

Even though the puzzler disassembles a complete puzzle, he invariably complains that there are too few or too many pieces when assembling the same puzzle. To avoid this complaint, each of the diagrams were checked and rechecked against the pieces of each puzzle so the reader can rest assured that the puzzle is complete in every detail.

As in all diagrams of this type of puzzle the dark sections represent cut away or removed portions. These removed sections are usually one half the thickness of the wood being used. All of the pieces have a front or top view and a side view. By having both views the maker of the puzzle should not experience any difficulties in construction.

The Design Puzzles

The gun, motorcycle, auto, plane, dog, ship, and tank puzzles are very difficult to construct because if the pieces are out of proportion the object which the puzzle represents will not be recognized and furthermore the puzzle will not be assembled, so do take your time when making the pieces for the puzzles in this group. As stated in the introductory section make the cut away parts a trifle smaller, and then when fitting puzzle file away the part that binds. This puzzle demands tight fitting parts; if the pieces are loose fitting the puzzle will not look like the object that it is supposed to represent.

The dark portions represent cut away parts. Do not round the corners or edges of any piece. A round piece gives too many clues and therefore is no longer a puzzle.

Gun Puzzle

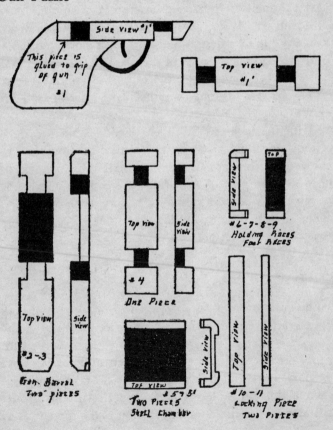

Motorcycle Puzzle

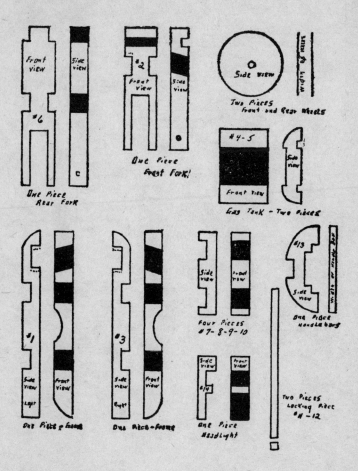

Automobile Puzzle

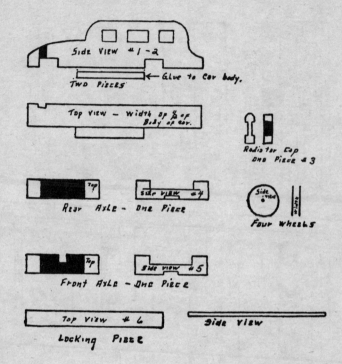

Side View #1-2

Two Pieces ← Glue to car body.

Top View — width of ½ of body of car.

Radiator Cap
One Piece #3

Rear Axle — One Piece

Top

Side View #4

Side view

Four Wheels

Front Axle — One Piece

Top

Side View #5

Top View #6

Side View

Locking Piece

Plane Puzzle

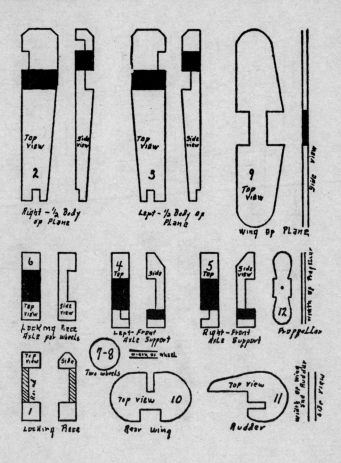

Dog Puzzle

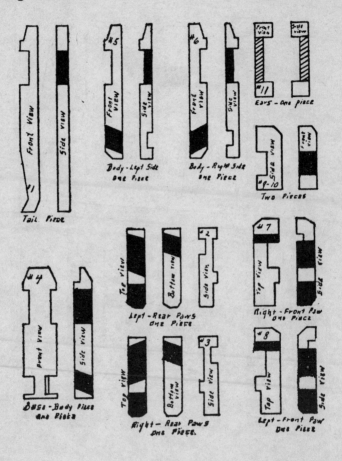

Ship Puzzle

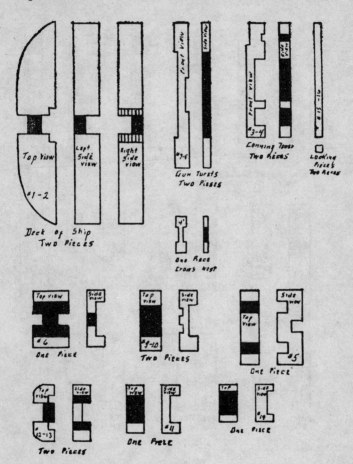

Tank Puzzle

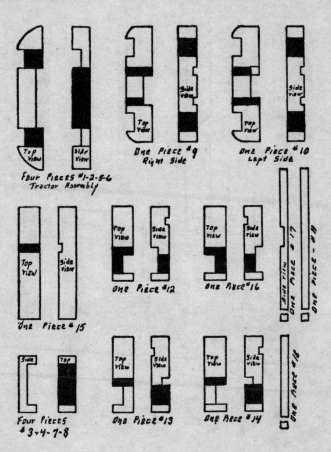

Four Pieces #1-2-5-6
Tractor Assembly

Top View
Side View

One Piece #9
Right Side

One Piece #10
Left Side

One Piece #15

One Piece #12

One Piece #16

One Piece #17

One Piece #11

Four Pieces
#3-4-7-8

One Piece #13

One Piece #14

One Piece #18

Cube and Burr Puzzles

The three puzzles in this group are simple to construct and with a diagram to consult, simple to assemble, but as so often stated: use the book to make a puzzle, but do not use it to solve the puzzle. There is more fun in solving than there is in having the puzzle solved.

When making this puzzle use the hard woods. Be accurate when making the pieces. Place pieces with similar cuts into a clamp or vise and file to exact size.

For the cube puzzle use different woods for each pair of pieces, and you will have a more colorful puzzle.

The burr puzzles are simple in construction but some individuals find them to be very difficult to assemble.

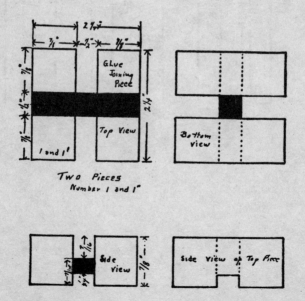

Cube Puzzle

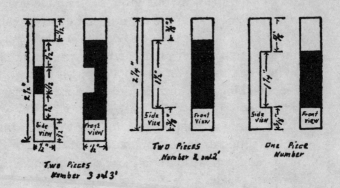

Two Pieces
Number 3 and 3'

Two Pieces
Number 2 and 2'

One Piece
Number

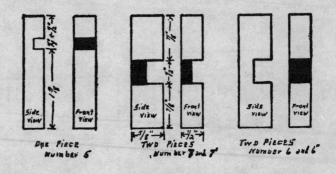

One Piece
Number 5

Two Pieces
Number 8 and 7'

Two Pieces
Number 6 and 6'

Cube Puzzle

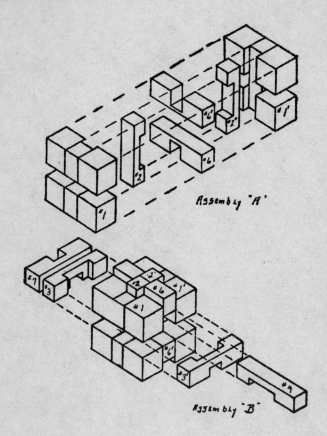

Assembly "A"

Assembly "B"

Cube Puzzle

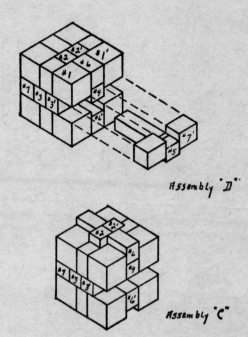

Burr Puzzle

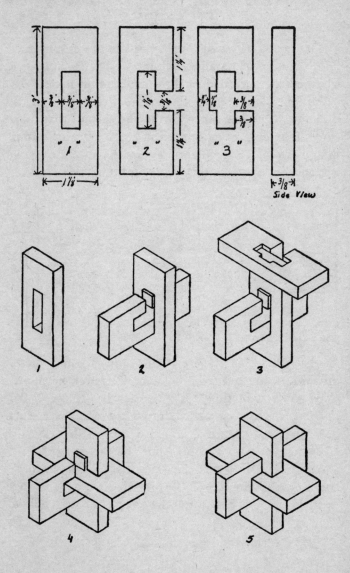

GEOMETRIC DESIGN PUZZLES

The geometric design puzzle is the oldest of puzzles. The Chinese Tangram, Archimedes puzzle and a host of others are recorded in the records of antiquity.

Although they have considerable historical significance yet time has not removed the shroud that makes three, four, five or more pieces of wood cut into simple designs from being puzzles. Today they are as fascinating and annoying as they were to the ancients.

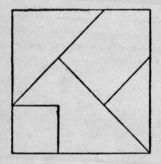 

The puzzles included in this unit are not merely drawn in a hit and miss manner. These ten have withstood the test of time and found to be tried and true puzzles. It is so very easy to draw a cross, a square, a star or a diamond shaped figure and then with scissors or knife to cut it up and say "put the pieces together to make a star." But that does not make a puzzle in the true sense of the word, because that jig saw arrangement is easily solved. Study the ten puzzles and you will discover that each one follows a geometric principle, axiom or rule. Usually two or more pieces are somewhat similar, but that similarity makes the puzzle difficult to solve. If you have a friend who is interested in

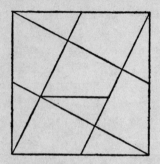 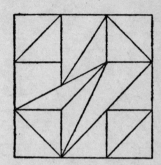

jig saw puzzles give him a star or diamond puzzle to solve and he will soon discover that he has a real puzzle and not a makeshift time killer.

For instance the cross puzzles look simple, but try number one on a friend, show him that it can be worked

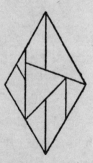 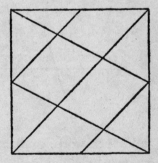

and hurriedly break it up. As a matter of fact construct a model, and, without studying the diagram, try to assemble it in a minute or two. This one is really the best cross puzzle available. The others are very good but they cannot be demonstrated.

When making these puzzles use ply wood or wood that is at least ½ inch in thickness. Paint the pieces to

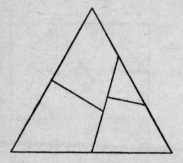

hide the grain markings. You will find that an assortment of this type of puzzle is very entertaining. The diamond and star puzzle retain the puzzle feature for a long time because no matter how proficient one becomes in assembling it, time removes that mental imprint and

unless you work it rather often you will find that it can be used indefinitely.

These ten puzzles make marvelous mitre box projects for the boy taking manual training, or for the boy who has nothing to do on rainy or stormy days.

For the best results in making this puzzle, make it out of cardboard then using these as models make the puzzle out of plywood, wood, or other solid object. When making the puzzle construct it large enough in width, length and thickness so that the pieces can be handled easily. A good rule to keep in mind is, that a puzzle which is easily handled is more fascinating, and less discouraging.

MISCELLANEOUS PUZZLES

The puzzles in this group are of a challenging type, and are my favorites. The coat hanger and coin puzzle is a good stunt, trick, or puzzle for the parlor, office, shop or other place where good fellows meet. The glass tube is a dandy parlor puzzle, and the nut and bolt puzzle is the best man sized puzzle on the market. Try the bolt puzzle on any man and you will be repaid a million fold for the efforts expended in making it. The cube puzzles will make marvelous gifts for the bedridden friend, and for the youngster who likes to do things with blocks.

These ten puzzles have withstood the test of time, and have proven themselves to be true recreation devices, make a set and you too will say, "The simplest in construction yet best of all."

Rearrange the Numbers Puzzle

Materials and method of constructing the numbers puzzle. Construct the puzzle out of apple box wood. Cut one piece 3¾ inches by 2½ inches. Along the outer edges of this rectangular block, tack or glue ½ inch strips of wood so that you have a miniature box. Out of apple box wood or linoleum make 24 ½ inch square blocks. Onto each of the blocks glue or carve the numbers one to twenty-four. To make for easier handling of the blocks place little eyelets, screws, or tacks into each of the blocks. Set up puzzle as shown in diagram.

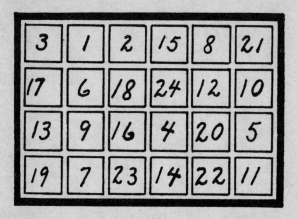

Puzzle: By exchanging one number for another, re-arrange the numbers into numerical sequence. The puzzle is to be solved in the least number of moves.

Solution for the Numbers Puzzle

MOVE BLOCKS NUMBERED (READ DOWN):

3 to 1	8 to 5
2 to 3	6 to 8
15 to 4	21 to 6
16 to 15	23 to 21
17 to 7	22 to 23
20 to 7	14 to 22
24 to 10	9 to 14
11 to 24	18 to 9
12 to 11	

Solved in 17 moves

Four Ace Cube Puzzle

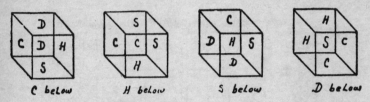

C below   H below   S below   D below

Puzzle: The object of the puzzle is to have four cubes in a straight line each touching the other, and these to be so arranged that there be four aces on each of the four exposed sides. They need not be arranged in the same order but they must all have a heart, club, spade and diamond exposed. This puzzle is not very simple so don't lose patience, stay with it until you solve it. It does make a dandy puzzle for the sick and bedridden.

Materials and methods of constructing the Four Ace puzzle. Make four one inch cube blocks. Now take an old deck of cards and cut out six of the hearts, diamonds, clubs and spade designs. Glue these designs on to the cubes as per diagram. When the pieces are glued and dried, close this book and you are ready to solve the puzzle.

Solution for Four Ace Puzzle.

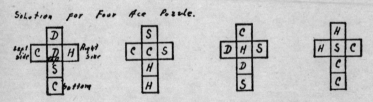

Solution for the Four Ace Cube Puzzle

The solution of the puzzle is shown in diagram. To make it more interesting change it into a four colored block puzzle by converting the aces into colors.

The Eight Cube Puzzle

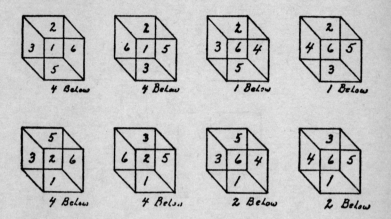

This is similar to the four ace puzzle, except that it is a more difficult and more exasperating puzzle.

Materials and method of constructing the Eight Cube puzzle. Make eight one inch cube blocks, or if you have a child around the house confiscate eight of his or her building blocks. If you are not so situated purchase a set of blocks from the five and ten cent store. Now either paint the numbers one to six on cubes as per diagram or substitute colors for each of the numbers. The object of the puzzle is to make a 2 inch cube out of the eight 1 inch cubes, so that each of the six outer sides are of one color or if you are using a number or letter in place of color, so that each of the six outer sides have four of a kind exposed.

Use this puzzle as a "Follow up" of the four ace puzzle. In fact it is advisable where and when possible to use the "Follow up" or progression theory of play in all of your puzzle activities. Don't carry a pocket full of

puzzles, use one at a time, and when you and your
friends have that one mastered, follow up the interest
created with another puzzle of the same type.

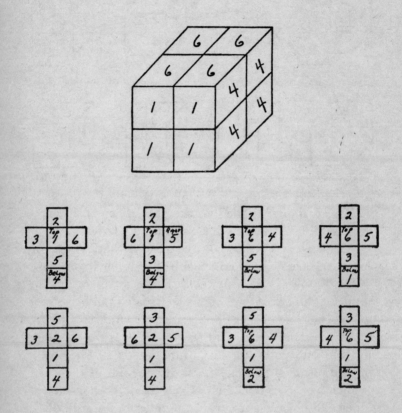

The Magic Square Puzzle

The magic square puzzle is a popular paper and
pencil leisure time killer, but early in the course of my
recreational experiences I discovered that even though
paper and pencil games were favorite diversions yet when

used as playground material, they did not carry-over for any period of time. To overcome that obstacle, the magic square games or problems were converted into a mechanical puzzle and were found to be very practical and satisfactory as puzzles.

One need not make a container for this puzzle, nor is it necessary to use numbered wood blocks, but as so often stated in this book—if you want to get the best possible results out of the puzzles herein described use wood or other solid objects to make the required parts. The mere sight of a container with numbered blocks creates an immediate interest and is in itself an advertisement so that you do not have to do any demonstrating or encouraging, instead of selling the leisure moment, it will be sold with the query "What's that?" or "May I try this or that puzzle?"

Therefore, to construct the magic square puzzle make a container out of apple box wood. Size of container is dependent upon the size of wood blocks used. However, if you make the blocks ½ inch square then cut a piece of apple box wood so that it measures 3¼ inches square. Along the outer edge nail or glue ½ inch wide apple box wood strips. On the base of the container, pencil mark thirty-six ½ inch squares. When box is marked and built apply shellac or varnish.

While container is drying, make thirty-six ½ inch square wood blocks. On one side of each block paint or carve out the numbers 1 to 6, making six blocks of each number. When carving is complete, fill the notches with a wood filler or plastic. When filler is dry apply varnish and numbers will be very conspicuous.

If you intend to use the puzzle for recreational play purposes do not glue paper numbers on the blocks because paper not only wears but it is very difficult to keep such blocks clean and neat.

Although the puzzle can be worked without any additional accessories yet for easier movement and manipulation of the wood blocks, it is advisable to place screws or tacks into center of blocks, but as stated previously this accessory is not necessary.

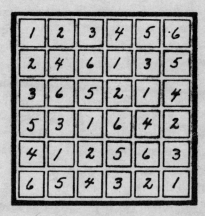

If you find that the 36 block magic square is losing face as a recreational device, increase the number of blocks to multiples of 7-8-9 and 10. If you do this you will find that the magic square puzzle is good for a summer playground or camp session.

The puzzle is to arrange the numbered blocks in the container in such positions, so that no more than one set of six numbers be in any one straight line, horizontally or vertically.

Bolt and Washer Puzzle

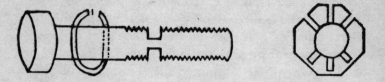

Puzzle: Remove the washer from the puzzle bolt.

Materials and method of constructing the bolt and washer puzzle. One ½ inch by 3 inch standard bolt with hexagon nut. Six ⅛ inch steel ball bearings. One 9/16 metal washer.

Method of constructing the puzzle bolt. If you have a metal lathe this puzzle will be a dandy project to fool with. Yes "Fool with" because the construction is not as easy as it appears to be. Therefore, if one craftsman may advise another, do not use a tempered or hard steel bolt, and when making the cut or notch into bolt use a good cutting tool. If you do not have access to a lathe, the price of having a bolt cut as per design is not very exorbitant and therefore have the bolt cut; you'll find that the investment will bring good returns.

The notch in the bolt is ¼ inch in width and ¼ inch in depth.

The six holes in the nut are made in the following manner. Drill three of the holes directly through three of the six hexagonal nut sides. The holes on the other three sides are continuations of the three holes, however they are not drilled completely through the sides. When holes have been drilled, partially plug two of the holes with small metal plugs. To do this efficiently plug part of holes with wood and then solder the remaining portion of the hole. When solder is hard the wood plugs can be dug out with a needle or other pointed object. When holes are plugged, screw nut onto bolt until unplugged hole is directly over bolt notch. Now through the unplugged hole pass the six $\frac{1}{8}$ inch steel ball bearings. Now seal or plug the hole with a metal plug or solder. When hole is plugged file the three hexagonal sides so that the plugs are not too conspicuous. Now unscrew the nut. If you constructed the bolt and nut accurately you should not be able to remove the nut. However if you hold the bolt parallel with your body, with head of bolt on top, the nut should be removable. If you are having difficulties tap the bolt slightly to ease the tension on the bearings. If the nut begins to unscrew make a few notches into the last or first thread on bolt, this because nut must not come off of bolt entirely. If it does you will have to be either a contortionist or you will have to remove one of the plugs and proceed to assemble puzzle as previously directed. When notch of bolt is exposed pass washer whose notch has been made slightly larger than original notch, over bolt notch and onto bolt. Now turn nut back onto bolt and over notch and you can now hand it to your pal with the request: "Remove the washer from the bolt."

Four Peg Brahma Puzzle

Materials and method of constructing the four peg Brahma puzzle: To construct this puzzle use apple box wood. Cut one piece 2 inches wide by $8\frac{3}{4}$ inches long. Subdivide it according to the diagram into four equal parts. At points marked off place wooden pegs by glueing them into base. Make pegs ¼ inch by 2½ inches in length. Paint each peg a different color. Make eight wood discs, so that each one is a trifle smaller than the other. Through the center of each disc drill a ¼ inch hole. For effect paint each disc a different color. For ease in handling make discs at least ¼ inch in thickness. Set up puzzle as shown on diagram.

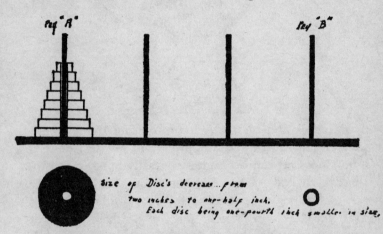

Puzzle: By using the pegs, transfer discs from peg "A" to peg "B." This transferring is done by moving one disc at a time to another peg and in such manner so that a small disc is on a larger disc. A large disc may never cover a small disc.

Solution for the Four Peg Brahma Puzzle

When solving this puzzle work with but four discs at a time, that is move discs 1 to 4 to peg "D" then move discs 5-6-7-8 in such a manner so that they be arranged accordingly on peg "B." When these four are properly placed and arranged, work with discs 1-2-3-4.

If you so desire you may increase the number of discs but always add an even number, never an odd number.

Three-Sided Pyramid Puzzle

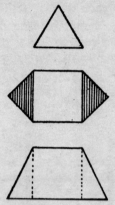

Materials and method of constructing the Pyramid puzzle: This puzzle requires a piece of wood made into a 60° block. It can be made very easily but before proceeding to make a 60° block of wood, make a guide out of cardboard or sheet metal. If a protractor is not available draw a circle on a piece of cardboard or sheet metal. Subdivide the circle into three parts, attach the points and your 60° guide can be made by removing one of the segments.

When you have the guide made, take a 3 inch wood block and with a pocket knife or spoke shave cut it into a three sided block. When you have the block roughly cut into a three sided piece use a wood file or plane or both to make it accurate. If you want a good pocket trick and do not object to investing a few cents for it, then it is advisable to have a 60° wood strip made in a mill work shop, because it is cheaper to have the wood cut to required size than to do the job without proper tools.

When you have the three sided wood strips made, proceed to construct the puzzle as per diagram. Use a 60° guide to mark lines where cut is to be made. To make an accurate puzzle, make cuts just a trifle beyond lines, then either file or sandpaper the 60° saw cut. Make two such pieces, the size of them depends upon size of material used.

If the two blocks are accurately made, place the bottom or square parts together in a perpendicular manner and you will have a three sided pyramid.

When trying this on your friends, do not permit the puzzler to lay the puzzle down. Demand that it be worked while being held. Reason being that when the puzzle is lying down the solution is more easily visualized.

Dime and Coat Hanger Puzzle

This puzzle is a trick rather than a puzzle, but it is included here because nine out of ten people are puzzled by it and will call it a puzzle. The materials required are as follows:

Any kind of wire coat hanger, but for the best performance use a hanger whose rung is perfectly straight and whose ear has a perfect coat hanger curve. If the hanger does not have those two qualities you'd better not try this puzzle.

Place the coat hanger on the first notch of your left or right index finger. Right or left depending on whether you are a right- or left-handed individual. When you have it so placed practice twirling the hanger around the finger. When you feel that you have mastered the twirl find an old and worn ten cent piece. It is very necessary to use an old and worn coin; you may be lucky with a new coin, but for best results use an old coin. Now hold the edge of the coin with thumb and index finger and place coin by balancing it on the center point of the lower rung as shown in diagram. Don't lose patience, "If at first you don't succeed, try, try again." When coin is balanced begin to move the hanger into a right and left swaying motion. When it is swaying with sufficient momentum begin twirling the hanger about your index finger. Again I say "If at first you don't succeed, try, try again."

This is a dandy puzzle to use anywhere, any place, and at any time, and all that is required is a coat hanger, any kind of coin and plenty of patience.

The solution to it is—Centrifugal force.

Glass Tube and Ball Balance Puzzle

Puzzle: Balance the two balls on wire suspension bridge.

Materials and method of constructing the tube and ball balance puzzle. To make the puzzle, obtain a six inch piece of heavy glass tubing one inch in diameter. Do not use thin glass tubing. Through two rubber or cork stoppers drill two holes to fit size of wire available. Place one of the stoppers into one of the tube ends, through the two holes in the stopper place the wire to be used. Pull the wire through the tube to the other end. Put the two ends of the wire through the second rubber stopper. Place two ball bearings into tube. Put rubber stopper into other opening of tube. Now place a piece of metal under wire stopper loops. This piece of metal is used so that when pulling the wire taut it will not be pulled through the rubber stoppers. When the puzzle is set up pull the wires taut so as to have a wire suspension bridge. To avoid scratches or other injuries place a piece of tape over exposed ends of the wire bridge.

Glass Tube and Bar Puzzle

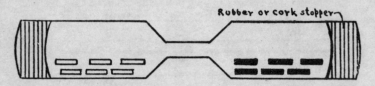

Materials and method of constructing the tube and bar puzzle: To make this puzzle purchase a few test tubes and with a Bunsen burner divide the tube at the center as shown in diagram. If you have not had any experience with glass heating and turning, you had better call upon some friend for assistance. If you would rather not try making the puzzle out of test tubes use two small bottles and connect their mouths with cork and glass or metal tubing. Inside of the small bottles place twelve one inch metal pegs with rounded ends, using six copper coated pegs and six natural colored pegs.

Puzzle: The object of the puzzle is to place the copper colored pegs on side marked for copper and the uncolored pegs on the uncolored side. The more pegs used the more interesting and difficult the puzzle.